INSIDE EGYPT

ALSO BY JOHN R. BRADLEY AND
AVAILABLE FROM PALGRAVE MACMILLAN

Saudi Arabia Exposed: Inside a Kingdom in Crisis

INSIDE EGYPT

THE LAND OF
THE PHARAOHS ON THE
BRINK OF A REVOLUTION

JOHN R. BRADLEY

First published in 2008 by
PALGRAVE MACMILLAN™
175 Fifth Avenue, New York, N.Y. 10010 and
Houndmills, Basingstoke, Hampshire, England RG21 6XS.
Companies and representatives throughout the world.

PALGRAVE MACMILLAN is the global academic imprint of the Palgrave Macmillan division of St. Martin's Press, LLC and of Palgrave Macmillan Ltd. Macmillan® is a registered trademark in the United States, United Kingdom and other countries. Palgrave is a registered trademark in the European Union and other countries.

ISBN-13: 978-1-4039-8477-7
ISBN-10: 1-4039-8477-8

Library of Congress Cataloging-in-Publication Data
Bradley, John R., 1970–
    Inside Egypt : the land of the Pharaohs on the brink of a revolution / John R. Bradley.
        p.   cm.
    Includes bibliographical references and index.
    ISBN 1-4039-8477-8
    1. Egypt—Politics and government—1952–1970. 2. Egypt—Politics and government—1970–1981. 3. Egypt—Politics and government—1981– 4. Egypt—Social conditions—1952–1970. 5. Egypt—Social conditions—1970–1981. 6. Egypt—Social conditions—1981–
I. Title.
DT107.83.B665   2008
962.05'5—dc22

                                                                            2007050070

A catalogue record of the book is available from the British Library.

Design by Letra Libre

First edition: May 2008
10 9 8 7 6 5 4 3 2 1
Printed in the United States of America.

CONTENTS

for Kelvin

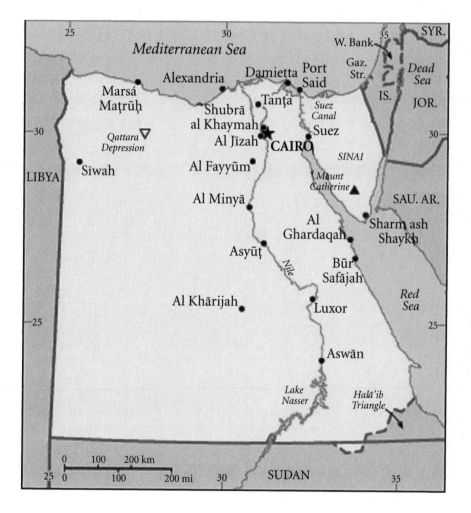

INSIDE EGYPT

CHAPTER ONE

A FAILED
REVOLUTION

A short walk from the American University in Cairo, through the bustling downtown streets of Africa's largest—and the Arab world's most populous—capital city, is a shabby little café called Al-Nadwa Al-Saqafiya. A hangout for Cairo's embattled community of liberal intellectuals, its wooden chairs and tables spill onto the street outside. The animated voices of customers compete with the constant honking of car horns; the orders operatically delivered by white-jacketed waiters are met with a chorus from nearby street vendors' repetitive cries. Smoke from the water pipes intermingles with exhaust fumes from the gridlocked traffic. It is a microcosm of contemporary Cairo: traffic congestion, noise pollution, and a social vibrancy created by a people who, despite the chaos engulfing them (or perhaps because of it), love nothing more than to engage in animated debate in public spaces about the trivial and the profound. In the winter of 2006, a movie called *The Yacoubian Building* was taking Egypt by storm as I made my way to Al-Nadwa Al-Saqafiya to meet up with Alaa Al-Aswany, author of the novel of the same name on which the movie was based. The most expensive Egyptian film ever produced, it features many of the country's established stars, and in its opening weeks broke all Egyptian box-office records. Set in a once-grand apartment block in the historic downtown district of Cairo, not far from Al-Nadwa Al-Saqafiya, the kaleidoscope of characters represent the various strata of Egypt's complex society. A central character is the building itself. It is a poor shadow of the splendor of its 1930s and 1940s' heyday, during what is known as Egypt's belle époque. The building's deterioration points to Egypt's own sad, steady fall from grace during the more than five decades of military rule since the July 1952 coup that overthrew the British-backed monarchy and brought to power Gamal Abdul Nasser and the Free Officers. With its near-barren cultural landscape, where the once-great but now heavily censored cinema industry churns out endless slapstick comedies, the movie exposes with unusual eloquence the grim reality that daily confronts Egyptians. Sexual decadence and political corruption permeate the world in which the characters move. Pimps, whores, petty tricksters, and professional con men with high connections vie for a share of the spoils of a declining nation now suffering the nightmare of a twin curse: free-fall privatization from above and the spread of Islamization from below. The rich in this portrayal of Egypt get ever richer, and the poor ever poorer. The middle class, meanwhile, has all but disappeared— and along with it any hope of social advancement based on a good education and a willingness to work hard. Radical Islamists prey on the vulnerable and the destitute abandoned by the system. The urbane and educated are trampled underfoot by mafia-like thugs known in Arabic as the "war rich"—better translated into English as "fat cats." This is a country from which almost all the young people long to escape, their last hope for a better future to leave their loved ones and travel in search of work and dignity.

***

Each Thursday Al-Aswany would meet up at Al-Nadwa Al-Saqafiya with friends, fellow intellectuals, and admirers of his novel to discuss the latest political and cultural developments in Egypt. Admirers he had aplenty. Even before the dramatic success of the movie made his name as an author internationally, *The Yacoubian Building* had been the best-selling novel in Egypt and the wider Arab world since its publication in 2002. Many had gone so far, somewhat prematurely, as to crown Al-Aswany the successor to Naguib Mahfouz, the great Egyptian author and Nobel Prize winner. Mahfouz, whose novels were also made into popular movies, died in a Cairo hospital in 2006 after a long illness following an assassination attempt in the early 1990s by an Islamist extremist, which had left him unable to write. In his late forties, with the neck and forearms of a prizefighter, Al-Aswany's name indicates that his family originates from the magnificent southern Egyptian city of Aswan, the Nubian heartland. His is an unpretentious, welcoming manner, suggesting (again like Mahfouz) that he had not let his newfound fame go to his head. He has lived in America and France, and is fluent in English, Spanish, and French, in addition to his native Arabic. A dentist by profession, he set up his first practice in the eponymous building in downtown Cairo that is fictionalized in the novel. Oddly for a dentist, but like most of the Egyptian men I have met, he is a chain-smoker. As I introduced myself, to break the ice he cracked a joke about cross-cultural integration—the theme of his latest novel, *Chicago*—after noticing that I smoke the local brand Cleopatra while he clutched two packets of his preferred American cigarettes.

There were about fifty people gathered at the coffee shop that chilly evening in the winter of 2006. I sat in the back row, an observer rather than a participant. They passed around a microphone hooked up to an amplifier that allowed each to be heard above the traffic din outside. The discussion, which Al-Aswany opened with a short speech, was dominated by the fallout from a recent comment by Culture Minister Farouk Hosni. He had said that the wearing of the veil, ubiquitous in Egypt since the early 1990s and resisted now only by the country's Coptic Christian minority, was a sign of "backwardness." The backlash against Hosni had been as tedious as it was merciless, proving nothing more, it struck me, than the validity of his assertion. Muslim Brotherhood MPs joined those of President Hosni Mubarak's own ruling (and ostensibly secular) National Democratic Party, which dominates the legislative assemblies formed on the back of what many, including the opposition, claim are fixed elections, in calling for Hosni's resignation. Columnists in pro-government and opposition newspapers alike launched vicious *ad hominem* attacks on the culture minister. Some suggested slyly (and with no apparent reason) that a man who seemed to have little interest in women should be the last person to express a strong opinion on what they were wearing. On the surface, this may seem an unlikely alliance of Islamist and secular forces, not least since the regime is routinely accused of imprisoning and torturing opposition activists and persecuting without mercy especially the fundamentalist Muslim Brotherhood. However, looked at more closely, the reaction to Hosni's comments nicely illustrates how the regime is stealing the clothes of the Islamists to shore up its ever-dwindling support among the masses. It is a practice that not incidentally has the benefit of pushing progressive voices still farther to the margins while bolstering an "Islamist threat" the regime plays up to help keep pressure and criticism from its paymasters in Washington to a minimum.

The comments expressed by those who had come to speak at Al-Aswany's informal salon were almost all supportive of the culture minister—not necessarily about his views on the veil, but certainly that he did not deserve to be attacked. This revealed both their liberal inclinations and also how out of touch they were with mainstream public opinion. After all, if both the opposition and the governing party saw benefits in making political hay from Hosni's comments, they both believed that the issue resonated among the people and could thus be manipulated for political gain. What the café's participants particularly could not understand was how an opinion expressed almost offhandedly by an individual, however prominent his position in government, could cause such a furor while stories of widespread poverty, massive unemployment, endemic corruption, and a universal culture of nepotism—the themes of Al-Aswany's novel—failed to stir the masses to anything approaching the same extent. The reaction proved to them the bankruptcy of domestic cultural discourse and the Islamists' hold over the collective Egyptian psyche. But it also demonstrated the almost naïve sense of justice on the part of those attending the salon, as the furor over the veil diverted attention from the grim reality the people faced but can do little about. It is no coincidence that slapstick comedies and manufactured umbrage have great prominence when pressing issues are depressingly unsolvable.

"I was raised here in downtown Cairo. I believe it's not so much a part of the city as an era that existed for more than a hundred and fifty years before the revolution, when Egypt was very tolerant," Al-Aswany told me after the crowd dispersed and we sat at an outside table.

For the liberal Egyptian elite from which Al-Aswany has emerged as a key figure, the different architectural styles that punctuated Cairo's landscape before the revolution stood for more than just the changing times and tastes. They represented a period going back to the early nineteenth century when Muslims, Christians, Jews, Egyptians, Ottomans, Armenians, Italians, and French lived and worked together in Egypt. The cityscape became a model of heterogeneity. This cosmopolitan past is accentuated in *The Yacoubian Building,* where the eponymous building, which stands as a faded art-deco block in real-life Cairo, is transformed into a relic of "the high classical European style" complete with columns and Greek visages in stone.

Al-Aswany was himself exposed to the West at a young age. He has said that a part of him is "essentially liberal." His father was a writer and artist, and Al-Aswany enjoyed a bookish and freethinking upbringing. "Whoever wanted to pray, prayed; whoever wanted to drink, drank; whoever wanted to fast, fasted," he told the local magazine *Egypt Today* during the publicity blitz surrounding the launch of *The Yacoubian Building.* He was eager to point out to me that he should not be identified with any particular character in the novel. Indeed, his main strength as a writer is his Proustian ability to show empathy with the contrasting viewpoints of his myriad characters. At the same time, it became obvious as our chat continued that he shared with his novel's elderly aristocratic hero, Zaki Pasha, a disdain for the drab reality of contemporary Cairo life, and a certain nostalgia for the prerevolutionary period—all heavily qualified by his reservations about the British colonialism that defined it.

"Colonialism is always bad. Whatever positive consequences it has are not created for the benefit of the indigenous peoples. But it's a fact that before the revolution we had our tolerant interpretation of religion in Egypt, and that's why we were so cosmopolitan—we had people from every corner of the earth living here," he reflected, before being politely interrupted by another group of fans asking him to sign English and Arabic editions of his book.

Al-Aswany had previously worked at a newspaper called *Al-Shaab,* "The People," where he was responsible for the literary page. The paper itself has an interesting history; having once been leftist it moved toward an increasingly Islamic character that presumably helps explain why Al-Aswany no longer works there. A generous interpretation of the paper's shift is that it sought to accurately reflect the sentiment of the people its name claimed to represent; a pragmatic variant might suggest sales were likely to be better once the leftist slant was eliminated. In reality, the shift was due to a loss of faith, so to speak, in leftist answers among its leading lights. It led an earlier hysterical campaign against the Culture Ministry for printing a novel called *A Banquet for Seaweed* also deemed un-Islamic by the local thought police. Al-Aswany may have felt some personal sympathy for Culture Minister Farouk Hosni's latest clash with the extremists on the issue of the veil (which the minister survived because he is friendly with the president's wife, Suzanne, who refuses to wear it). For he, too, had been on the receiving end of a similarly ferocious smear campaign in the pro-government newspapers. Columnists accused him of "tarnishing Egypt's image abroad" (officially a crime)—not least because one of his characters is a fairly openly gay man (homosexuality is quite common among Egyptian youths, but the subject is not normally discussed frankly); and one scene in the novel describes the brutal rape of an Islamist suspect by a government-hired thug in one of the country's police stations, where the rape of men and women as a degrading punishment and a method of extracting confessions is routinely alleged.

Egyptians are the most patriotic people in the Arab world. This may not seem consistent given that I have never come across a local who does not despise his president to one degree or another, and that an international Pew poll in July 2007 found that a staggering 87 percent of Egyptians (the largest majority of all the thirty-seven countries surveyed) were dissatisfied with the performance of their government. At the same time, it is hard to find anyone who does not love his country, take great pride in its past, and have great faith in its people's potential if given half a decent stab at their future. The key to understanding this apparent contradiction is the recognition that while well aware of their country's shortcomings, Egyptians nevertheless resent it when outsiders bring attention to them, and even more so when fellow Egyptians wash their collective dirty laundry in public for the benefit of a Western audience already perceived as being bombarded by negative images of the Arab world.

I reminded Al-Aswany of this before I read back to him what he had said about Egypt in the same interview with *Egypt Today* in response to a devastating survey of the country by Mondial, a leading U.K. provider of advice for foreign companies investing in Egypt and for those seeking travel insurance. The survey had produced a wave of soul-searching in the Egyptian media, and not a few knee-jerk reactions, after it ranked the country's service and tourist sectors a flat zero. "It has reached a point where we have reached zero," Al-Aswany told the publication. "The zero we received by Mondial is a fair result, very fair, not only in the Mondial, but in everything. That zero really should not be given to the Egyptians; it should be given to the Egyptian government. The Egyptian government should get a zero in all fields, not only in soccer, but in health and education, in democracy, and in everything." When I asked him about his responsibility as an Egyptian for the way the country is perceived by outsiders, the principal readers of *Egypt Today,* he merely shrugged and said: "It's not my job as a novelist to ensure that millions of tourists visit Egypt every year." In any case, he added, he was certain that the lackeys writing the columns against him in the state-owned media had been rewarded handsomely by the government for expressing their "opinions." It was this reality, he said, that should be the cause of national shame. The reception he received from ordinary Egyptians as he walked the streets of Cairo proved to him that at the grassroots level many appreciated his efforts. Finally, he returned with a sigh to his central theme: "The problem with Nasser's rule was that it set up a system that was fundamentally undemocratic, which we still have to this day."

As though to prove his point, on the Thursday of the week after I met him the secret police arrived at Al-Nadwa Al-Saqafiya shortly before the salon was about to get under way. The owner was informed that the gathering was illegal, the waiters were roughed up and ordered to stop serving the guests drinks, and the electricity supply was eventually cut by the terrified owner (a friend of Al-Aswany's for more than a decade). From that day on, this little dissenting group of freethinkers would have to find somewhere else to express their personal opinions. Al-Aswany seems to have escaped arrest (the fate of many lesser-known liberal intellectuals, bloggers, and opposition political activists) only because his international fame had grown to the extent that the regime, under limited pressure from Washington and international watchdogs over its appalling human rights and democracy record, had presumably decided that the inevitable outcry in the global media over such an act of awful silencing would prove more trouble than it was worth. Anyway, all but the most ruthless dictatorships know that there is some benefit to be gained by leaving a few prominent liberals to their own devices. They create for the outside world a false impression of domestic freedom and plurality.

"Nasser was the worst ruler in the whole history of Egypt." So remarks the hero of *The Yacoubian Building*, Zaki Pasha, whose father was a member of the aristocracy that was swept from power in 1952, in a memorable section of the novel. The movie, for the most part, was a faithful adaptation of the novel, the regime's attitude toward Nasser's legacy and followers having evolved to the extent of permitting tolerance of dissent. However, perhaps signifying the limits still observed when it comes to direct, stinging criticism of Nasser in more popular media such as film, that statement was omitted from the movie. So was Zaki Pasha's heartfelt elaboration on it in the novel's pages: "He ruined the country and bought us defeat and poverty. The damage he did to the Egyptian character will take years to repair. Nasser taught the Egyptians to be cowards, opportunists, and hypocrites." Asked by Buthayna, his young and impoverished sweetheart (who also deeply laments the legacy of the revolution), why Nasser is still loved, Zaki Pasha barks contemptuously: "Anyone who loves Nasser is either an ignoramus or did well out of him. The Free Officers were a bunch of kids from the dregs of society, destitutes and sons of destitutes. . . . They ruled Egypt and they robbed it and looted it and made millions."

<hr />

The Yacoubian Building was the most prominent example of an ongoing cultural reassessment in Egypt of the 1952 revolution and contrariwise of the prerevolutionary ancien régime, for so long dismissed by the education curriculum and government-controlled media as colonialist and so evil per se. The hugely charismatic Nasser, it is true, was worshipped by the Egyptian masses until his death in 1970. In a way, it is not hard to understand why. There were considerable short-term benefits of Nasser's rule: the final liberation of Egypt from foreign dominance; the expansion of the education system; guaranteed civil service jobs for university graduates;

the nationalization of the Suez Canal and building of the High Dam; fairer land redistribution. To say that the Free Officers were the "dregs of society" might be something of an exaggeration; they certainly understood how exploiting resentment of the rich (many of whom technically were foreign) and providing benefits to the poor would generate support. Perhaps most important to understanding Nasser's appeal was the sense of pride he gave many Egyptians. This is notwithstanding the fact that he betrayed them when Israel obliterated the Egyptian air force in a matter of hours at the start of the 1967 war while the Nasser-funded Voice of the Arabs radio station in Cairo broadcast outlandish claims of a stunning Egyptian victory. However, even what were considered the short-term benefits of Nasser's rule are now a distant, troubled memory for all but the regime itself and a small band of die-hard intellectuals aligned with various Nasserite parties and publications. Now anniversaries of the revolution are a time for lamentation rather than celebration, if they are marked at all, regardless of a lingering appreciation, on a sentimental level, for Nasser as an inspirational pan-Arab, anticolonialist, and anti-Zionist leader. On the day-to-day level, a deep sense of stagnation instead pervades as Egyptian society implodes and the regime abdicates Egypt's historic role as leader of the Arab world. As the *Economist* magazine, which covers Egypt more astutely than any other Western publication, wrote on the fiftieth anniversary of the coup, the country "is not in the mood for fun." Its economy and politics are stalled, the *Economist* added, "with strife in the surrounding region stunting hopes of relief anytime soon. Even so, the Egyptian government has lumbered into action with pageantry, parades, and speeches. . . . The fanfare is meant to boost national pride. But it seems instead to have added to the unease of a country that has grown unhappy with both itself and the outside world."

What was the reality of Nasser's revolutionary regime? An objective assessment can only draw one conclusion: It led Egypt to military catastrophe abroad while mocking its own grand declarations of democracy and dignity for all at home. Nasser was thirty-four years old at the time of the coup and had visited only one other Arab country, Sudan, before coming to power. He knew few Iraqis, Syrians, or Palestinians personally. The basis of his vision of pan-Arab unity, in other words, was a fallacious dream. It evaporated once it encountered reality in the form of attempted or aborted alliances with other Arab countries, most famously Syria. However, the cumulative effect of his military coup would still have disastrous long-term consequences for the wider Arab region. As Laura M. James sums it up in *Nasser at War: Arab Images of the Enemy* (2006): "Nasser's coup would inspire a series of inferior imitations by cells of 'Free Officers' across the Arab world—in Iraq, a bloodbath; in Yemen, a façade; in Libya, a farce." Nasser's decision to fight a proxy war against Saudi Arabia in Yemen in the 1960s, sending thirty thousand of Egypt's best soldiers to the southern Arabian tribal country and thus leaving Egypt defenseless in 1967, was not only a tactical military miscalculation; it was also strikingly hypocritical, coming from a man who had railed against foreign interference in his own country, and who would place pan-Arab unity at the top of his foreign policy agenda. Then again, hypocrisy was a trademark Nasser characteristic from the outset. If the CIA was not behind the "anti-imperialist" coup, it certainly had foreknowledge of it. Nasser then proved himself perfectly willing to work with the Americans until they turned against him. Even his celebrated land reform laws formed a key part of a U.S. foreign policy strategy at the time, which aimed to prevent the regional spread of communism.

Back in Egypt, Nasser, like a petty village leader, promoted his cronies according to their personal loyalty rather than on their merits. Abdel Hakim Amer is the most infamous example. Made Egypt's chief of staff and subsequently Nasser's first vice president, Amer proved incompetent beyond measure. Nasser got rid of him only after his military advice, based on fanciful speculation and an eternal eagerness to please his old friend rather than risk offending him by bringing home ugly truths, led Egypt to defeat in 1967. The officers around Nasser, Amer, and other coup leaders had quickly formed circles of power that put all their efforts into the wrestling match for control that ensued. These new corrupt elites had none of the positive attributes of the former decadent, but culturally sophisticated, aristocracy they had replaced and humiliated. From their new positions of power, they did what such people have ever done: trade on their influence, extort their share of every import and export deal from arms to lemons, and profit from appropriations (read: theft) of real estate—all in the name of the republic and its people.

That was just the beginning. The press, which had enjoyed considerable freedom for more than a half century under the British-backed monarchy, was nationalized in 1960 after years of coercion. The loyal "editors in chief" Nasser personally appointed to established newspapers became more royal than the royals. Mohammed Hassanein Heikal, made editor of the biggest-selling daily, *Al-Ahram*, founded in the mid-nineteenth century, would emerge as the most famous Egyptian journalist. His weekly Friday column was essential reading for those eager to know what Nasser himself was thinking. This fact alone is a terrible indictment of the print media of the period. Heikal, many claimed, was little more than Nasser's chief propagandist and censor, no matter how elegant a phrase he could turn out. He and the other editors were accused of cutting out the heart of Egypt's great dailies. The official government-run papers continue to be published today with the obligatory front-page banner headline celebrating Mubarak's latest inane pronouncement on domestic or international issues only because an arbitrary government injection of funds and a near-monopoly on advertising keeps them afloat.

Nasser banned the opposition political parties that had similarly thrived in prerevolutionary Egypt. The results were equally disastrous. A one-party system was introduced. It ensured a military monopoly of political power, with Nasser, who never stood for election, emerging supreme after a bitter internal power struggle with the republic's first leader, General Mohammed Naguib. Executive agencies set up to maintain checks and balances in the revolution's aftermath were, like the newspaper columnists, easily intimidated. They, too, failed to offer substantive criticism of the coup plotters' excesses. An extensive security and intelligence apparatus was put in place to spy on and control the masses that put to shame even the spy network of King Farouk, the last, sad monarch to rule, and cemented the officers' iron grip on power.

Tens of thousands of members of the Muslim Brotherhood (founded in 1928 as a grassroots charity organization with the aim of returning the masses to the fundamentals of Islam—as interpreted by the Brothers) were imprisoned and tortured by Nasser, dozens to their death. Perhaps the most famous was Sayyid Qutb, who in many ways laid the intellectual foundations for terrorism that would later come to plague Egypt and other countries throughout the Arab world and beyond. Those who survived the purge fled to temporary exile in the ultraconservative Gulf states. There they became immersed in the extremist Wahhabi ideology promoted by the Saudi ruling family. Wahhabism is alien to Egypt's tolerant, pluralistic traditions of Islam, but the Brothers would eventually bring it back with them when invited to return to the country in the 1970s by Anwar Al-Sadat to counter the Marxist opposition that had emerged to Nasser's rule. Many of the Muslim Brotherhood leaders who had remained at home were hanged. The long-term cultural consequences of this imported Wahhabism were tragic, especially for the country's minority Christians. They are damned—along with Jews and Sufis—as "infidels" by Wahhabi ideology, if not by official Muslim Brotherhood policy.

However, the extent to which the Free Officers were prepared to crush even nonradical, secular rivals in the name of the people's liberation was made evident when the leaders of a workers' protest were swiftly tried and executed in the months following the coup. The show trial sent a clear message to anyone who might dare to offer a voice of dissent.

Within a few years, then, Nasser had laid the foundations of a brutal police state ruled by a military dictatorship that selected someone from its own ranks as president with almost total power. Egypt has remained under some form of emergency law (which is to say military rule) for all but eight of the years since 1952. According to Amnesty International, eighteen thousand people are at present being held in Egypt without charge. A pledge in 2007 finally to do away with the emergency law was met with universal derision, because the regime introduced simultaneous changes to the constitution that made its worst aspects permanent. As that cynical maneuver shows, the Mubarak-led military regime is a devoted student of the Nasser school. This is manifested most obviously in its reluctance to risk losing power by making the country's institutions truly democratic and thus giving free rein to public opinion, especially now that public opinion often finds its noisiest expression (through the regime's own fault) in the sort of vicious hatemongering that Islamist fundamentalists everywhere substitute for genuine debate. The institutions are still largely run by figures who served their political apprenticeship in the regime prior to Nasser's death.

Leaving no doubt as to where his own personal loyalties lie, Mubarak described the revolution as "the crowning glory of the Egyptian people's struggle" when he marked its fiftieth anniversary in a speech to graduates of his alma mater: the Cairo Military Academy.

Thus, the mechanisms of this rotten authoritarian system established by Nasser remain intact to this day, despite more than fifty years of dramatic social and economic changes in Egypt. Unsurprisingly, a growing nostalgia for the period before the revolution that *The Yacoubian Building* masterfully tapped into has therefore emerged. Liberal, Western-oriented intellectuals and ordinary folk busy making ends meet alike now see it, however romantically, as a lost golden age. The evidence is all around. After the revolution the nonhereditary honorifics such as *pasha* (a high rank in the Ottoman empire political system) and *bey* (one rank lower than *pasha)* were banned, thereby signifying that traditional hierarchies and deference were no longer in play. These, however, have been revived, ironically used mostly by officialdom and the successors of the cadre of ministers, high-ranking officers, and undersecretaries who had sought to abolish all such "feudal" designations. The change in fortunes of such titles was made clear to me back in the 1990s. An elderly Egyptian woman who had moved to Australia shortly after the coup, but returned for the first time to help develop a curriculum at the Arabic language school where I was studying, took me aside after hearing me address a passing Egyptian I knew as pasha. She advised me earnestly: "He will get very angry if you use titles like that!" Later, I asked my teacher if this was true.

She chuckled as she explained that the old woman still appeared to be living in the Egypt of the 1950s.

The negative changes brought about by the coup are meanwhile the subject of an endless flow of books. One, by the respected Egyptian sociologist Galal Amin, *Whatever Happened to the Egyptians? Changes in Egyptian Society from 1950 to the Present,* laments the cultural, economic, and social deterioration of postrevolutionary Egypt by contrasting it with charming stories from the author's prerevolutionary childhood. It won a leading prize at the Cairo International Book Fair in 1998, and went on to sell so many copies in Arabic and English that Amin published a follow-up best-selling volume: *Whatever Else Happened to the Egyptians? From the Revolution to the Age of Globalization.* Amin is hardly alone. "I grew up in the last days of the British Empire. My childhood fell in that era when the words 'imperialism' and 'the West' had not yet acquired the connotations they have today," writes Leila Ahmed, a U.S.-based academic born to an upper-class Cairo family during the interwar years, in her memoir *Border Passage* (2000). One of many similar memoirs published in the West by Egyptians trying to reclaim their prerevolutionary past, *Border Passage* lyrically charts how many middle- and upper-class families saw no contradiction between their dedicated and often active nationalism and the fact that they were eager to entrust the task of raising their children, for instance, to Westerners, who presumably could hardly be relied on to encourage anticolonial feelings among their charges. Ahmed's book taps beautifully into a generation that grew up in a sophisticated and cosmopolitan society, where one's personal distinctiveness mattered as much as one's nationalist aspirations.

It was a time when Egyptian society's undoubted inequalities and exploitative political manipulation by outside powers were somehow tempered by the refined high culture of tolerance, cosmopolitanism, intellectualism, and architectural extravagance the outsiders imported and the Ottoman-descended aristocracy cultivated, and from which even the Egyptian nationalist movement itself would draw inspiration as it emerged in opposition to British rule in the late nineteenth century. Thus the great Egyptian nationalist leader Saad Zaghloul, whose forced exile by the British in 1919 would stir the masses into launching a mini-revolution that eventually led to partial sovereignty, could say temperately of the Westerners in his country: "I have no quarrel with them personally . . . but I want to see an independent Egypt." This controversial take on the prerevolutionary era portrays Egyptians as embracing the best of what the world had to offer; being less overtly religious than they are today, but more ethical; and correspondingly being more respectful of the true, underlying message of Islam that finds its expression in good deeds rather than in the mere observance of strict religious rituals and the endless issuance of obscure and often hateful fatwas. Islamic scholars of the time, eager to merge Islam with modernity and democracy, subjected even the Qur'an to rational inquiry and analysis.

Even King Farouk has been rehabilitated. In Ramadan/September 2007 a new televised miniseries charting the rise and fall of the king by focusing on his "human side" became the most popular program in the Arab world and in Egypt for those who had access to satellite television. The serial was produced by the Saudi-owned satellite channel MBC, and also aired on the equally popular Saudi-funded Orbit channel. But it was initially not shown on Egyptian national television, for which it was reportedly written some fifteen years earlier. The Egyptian government had refused to fund it on political grounds. It is difficult not to speculate that MBC's decision to produce it, despite Egyptian officials' efforts at hindrance by refusing to give the crew permission to film on location in the royal palaces and other real-life locations, might also have been at least partly political. Columnists at Saudi-funded newspapers wasted no time in holding up the supposed virtues of the monarch while praising their own Gulf dynasties, which survived Nasser's attempts to undermine them. Giving in to commercial pressure after the series proved one of the biggest Ramadan television hits in years, Egyptian TV announced that it would air a prime-time repeat.

After that fateful day of July 23, 1952, the "Paris Along the Nile," as Cairo was lovingly renamed by the foreigners who flocked to the city and helped to design, build, and run it during the nineteenth and early twentieth centuries, was cast into the proverbial dustbin of history. Quarrels rather than friendships between Egyptians and foreigners became the order of the day. Indeed, the foreigners' property was confiscated. Along with the aristocracy itself, they eventually either chose to leave or, after the 1956 Suez War, were forced to flee. Symbolic of Nasser's rank xenophobia was his expulsion of half of Egypt's Jews, endlessly linked in the regime propaganda machine with the recently created state of Israel. This was one of a number of witch hunts Nasser used (another targeting the Muslim Brotherhood) to deflect attention from his own shortcomings, especially in the area of foreign policy. In the case of the Jews, the process was hardly undermined by the bumbling efforts of the Jewish state itself in trying to recruit and fund a little band of Cairo Jews to carry out terrorist attacks in the city in a bid to foment social strife and political instability. Still, if a democracy is best judged by the protection it affords its religious and other minorities, the fact that only a handful of Jews remain in Egypt, while the words "Jew" and "Israeli" have become synonymous among Egyptians themselves in casual anti-Semitic conversation, speaks volumes about Nasser's "democratic" legacy, as does the fact that Cairo's main synagogue is now surrounded by twenty-four-hour security provided by the army.

The Arab-American scholar Fouad Ajami has said that at the heart of Egyptian life there now lies a terrible sense of disappointment. Ajami was widely respected as an observer of Arab political and cultural trends but has been criticized following his passionate advocacy of the ill-fated U.S.-led invasion of Iraq in 2003. In a characteristically nuanced essay on Egyptian nostalgia published in *Foreign Affairs* in 1995, he argued that the pride of modern Egypt has been far greater than its accomplishments, and that the dismal results are all around: "the poverty of the underclass, the bleak political landscape that allows an ordinary officer to monopolize political power and diminish all would-be rivals in civil society, the sinking of the country into sectarian strife between Muslim and Copt, the dreary state of its cultural and educational life." It is out of this disappointment, Ajami argued, that "a powerful wave of nostalgia" has emerged for the liberal interlude in Egyptian politics from the 1920s through the revolution of 1952, when Egypt was ruled by a parliamentary democracy and constitutional monarchy—for "its vibrant political life, for the lively press of the time, for the elite culture with its literati and artists, for its outspoken, emancipated women who had carved a place for themselves in the country's politics, culture, and journalism." Some of this "is the standard nostalgia of a crowded, burdened society for a time of lost innocence and splendor," he conceded, before adding: "some, though, is the legitimate expression of discontent over the mediocrity of public life." Egypt produced better, freer cinema in the "liberal age" than it does today, Ajami concluded, while "its leading intellectual figures were giants who slugged out the great issues of the day and gave Egyptian and Arabic letters a moment of undisputed brilliance."

This sense of hopelessness, and corresponding nostalgia, has deepened in the decade since Ajami's article appeared. "I don't believe the 1952 revolution had any positive features, since democracy is still missing," Awad Al-Mor, the former chief justice of the Egyptian Supreme Constitutional Court, said on the fiftieth anniversary of the coup. "The greatest failure of the revolution is the lack of democracy, which I believe led to our defeat in 1967. Egypt has never experienced a democratic government from 1952 until now. . . . The revolution embraced the slogan 'Raise your head, my brother, for the age of oppression is over,' but it replaced it with the heavy foot of Gamal Abdul Nasser, which kept people's heads down." That such criticism should come from a pillar of the post-Nasser establishment is at first glance baffling, although the judiciary has often proved to be a thorn in the regime's side: Nasser summarily sacked hundreds of leading judges who raised objections to his authoritarian rule. By 2006, in fact, the country's top judges, protesting en masse corrupt elections they were constitutionally authorized to supervise but had been prevented from monitoring effectively by the Mubarak regime, had become the unofficial leaders of a nationwide protest movement that drew on all segments of Egyptian society: secular intellectuals, students, labor activists, mainstream Islamists. For a while it seemed that the regime was collapsing from forces opposing its rule both within and without its direct spheres of influence, as Egypt witnessed the most widespread public disturbances since the years leading up to the revolution. This time, though, the strikers and demonstrators were rallying against the political stagnation and crude brutality of President Hosni Mubarak's rule. Like his predecessor (and successor of Nasser) Anwar Al-Sadat, Mubarak is a military man, the latest guardian of the corrupt, antidemocratic military establishment created by Nasser that still grips the country's civil society in its rusty vise.

However, while Nasser set strict personal limits on how far he was prepared to concede control of the country to the British and then the United States, nationalizing the Suez Canal in 1956 in a brilliant strategic move that effectively brought to an end British colonial dominance of Egypt and the wider region, these days Egypt under Mubarak is comparatively more dependent on the United States, the new imperial power broker in the region. The late Iraqi leader Saddam Hussein, who knew a thing or two about the way Arab despots engage in wheeling, dealing, and horse-trading in order to cling to power, once smartly observed of Mubarak that "he is like a pay phone. You deposit your money, and you get what you want in return." That the Egyptian regime continues to depend on the indulgence of America, which since a peace treaty was signed between Egypt and Israel in 1979 has provided some $2 billion in military aid annually (which some see as a bribe for maintaining a Cold Peace with the Jewish state), is an aggravating humiliation for ordinary Egyptians. For a start, they benefit not at all from the money as they see the gap between the rich and poor grow ever wider. Perhaps more crucially in a country where national pride is so deeply rooted, they also resent America's crude military adventurism in the region and their own leaders' complicity in it. This is not least because of their strong sympathy with the Palestinian cause, and the neoconservative-led invasion of Iraq is widely seen by Egyptians as having been launched at the behest of an Israel-allied cabal in Washington.

More than five decades after the coup, then, Egypt has come full circle. The same grievances that led the people to rebel, and the Free Officers to take advantage of that rebellion to seize power, are now at the root of new street protests and bitterly expressed articles in the emerging opposition media: an end to colonialism and its agents, and the domination of government by exploitative capitalists; an end to the disregard for social justice; and the need for a democratic system of governance that pays more than lip service to the demands of its people. With the president's suave, arrogant son Gamal Mubarak, crown prince–like, widely perceived as being groomed to take over the presidency from his ailing father, few can see any meaningful difference between the current regime and the monarchy it ousted five decades ago in the name of the liberation of the Egyptian people. The nostalgia for the monarchy is not that different from the fundamentalists' yearning for the purity of the time of the Prophet and his followers, a wistful desire for a time better than the present when the present is so dismal.

Even conceding the undoubted ill effects of direct or indirect colonial rule, the current Egyptian regime fares badly in every respect when compared to the prerevolutionary monarchy that Napoleon Bonaparte's short-lived invasion of Egypt in 1798 helped to create. Nasser's coup got rid of everything that was good in Egypt, and slowly replaced everything that was bad with something much worse. Napoleon's attempted conquest of Egypt, and the humiliation at the hands of Britain that ended it, inadvertently gave birth to the modern Egyptian nation-state. It would be developed throughout the nineteenth and early twentieth centuries along European lines under the leadership most notably of Mohammed Ali and his grandson, Khedive Ismail. Mohammed Ali is often referred to as the "founder of modern Egypt," and his descendants would rule the country with varying degrees of monarchical power until his great-great-grandson, King Farouk, was finally toppled by Nasser in 1952.

After the French left Egypt, the army of the Ottoman Empire, which had ruled from 1517, remained in the country, determined to prevent a revival of Mamluk power and autonomy and to bring Egypt under the control of the central government. An aristocracy of white slaves, the Mamluks had ruled Egypt as an independent state from 1250 until 1517, and then stayed on as Ottoman subjects to form the leading class in Egyptian society.

In the seventeenth century, however, they won back power. For two hundred years they replenished their ranks through the slave markets, while ruling through tyranny. In the chaos of Napoleon's departure, a third potential ruling class emerged. Caught up in the rivalry between the Mamluks and the Ottoman government, they were made up of an only nominally loyal Albanian contingent of Ottoman forces that had come to Egypt in 1801 to fight against the French. The contingent was led by Mohammed Ali himself, a mercenary who had arrived in Egypt as a junior commander in the Albanian forces. By 1803, he had risen to the rank of commander. After consolidating his power base, being elected governor by Cairo's powerful religious sheiks in 1805, and being granted the title of viceroy by the Ottomans, he made plans to eliminate his rivals. In March 1811, he did so in spectacular fashion, having sixty-four Mamluks—including twenty-four beys—assassinated after inviting them for an official ceremony. Thus he became the sole strongman in Egypt, and was afforded a unique opportunity to unite a country teetering on the brink of all-out anarchy.

One of Mohammed Ali's great ambitions included the eventual detachment of Egypt from the Ottoman Empire. However, he realized that to achieve this goal Egypt had to be strong economically and militarily. He courted the Europeans from the outset, giving away treasures to Paris and London while negotiating first with one power and then the other. The Ramses II obelisk stands in Paris's Place de la Concorde to this day, as does Cleopatra's Needle on the Thames Embankment in London. Working long hours and personally visiting his pet projects, he set about building new factories imported in kits from Europe, surrounded himself with clever European advisors, and steeped himself in the high technology of the time—laughing heartily, for instance, when shown how electricity worked by being given a shock with a live wire. He cultivated the most talented men he came across in Cairo, skillful and dedicated individuals with backgrounds as diverse as his own: Armenian migrants, Coptic financial experts. They formed a new bureaucracy and military that answered solely to him. The centralized rule, and the authority he had among his subjects, allowed this Macedonia-born Albanian to undertake important initiatives that laid the foundations of the Egyptian education system, revived cultural life, and reformed the agricultural system—the leader always looking to Paris for inspiration. Ideas about politics, society, and culture that emerged in subsequent generations date back to this period; but even by the end of his own reign, Egypt had a corps of technically trained bureaucrats and army officers committed to Westernizing reform and Egyptian autonomy.

Crucially, Mohammed Ali promoted the growth of cotton for export to the expanding cotton mills of Europe, revenues from which would fund an economic boom under his grandson Khedive Ismail, who ruled from 1863 until 1879. Thanks to a stoppage of American cotton imports during the 1861–1865 civil war, the price of Egyptian cotton soared as Britain looked ever more anxiously to Egypt to supply Leeds and Manchester. Flush with cash, Ismail began to realize more fully his grandfather's ambition of launching grand public works: canals, land reclamation, urban structures, and infrastructure. In one year alone he set about building four hundred and fifty bridges, sixty-four sugar mills, and almost one thousand miles of railway. He also established the General Postal Union, and telegraph wires were erected as far south as Sudan; soon Egypt could boast one of the most efficient postal services in the world. The country's image as a primitive backwater of the Ottoman Empire, ruled by a class of slaves, was finally shed forever, as architects, artists, politicians, and musicians were soon flocking to Cairo and the Mediterranean coastal city of Alexandria.

Ismail's visit to the Exposition Universelle in Paris's Champ-de-Mars in 1867 was a life-changing experience, and had especially dramatic consequences for Egypt. "My country is no longer in Africa; we are now part of

Europe," he famously declared soon afterward. He seized the opportunity of the opening of the Suez Canal in 1869 to build new districts in the European style, with magnificent parks and wide streets and palaces to accommodate his European guests—wanting to do for Cairo what Baron Georges Haussmann had done for Paris. He opened the doors of Egyptian society and economy to many Europeans, and after the British took control of the Egyptian treasury (and therefore by default the country) in 1882, following a financial crisis they effectively engineered, hundreds of thousands of Europeans flocked to Egypt and settled in Cairo and Alexandria in search of fame and fortune. They established their own quarters and founded and operated Western-style institutions. Ismail had literally laid the foundations in Cairo, paving streets and long roads and building gardens, museums, apartment blocks, theaters, French-style fountains, and a world-class opera house (Verdi's *Aida*, with a scenario written by Mariette Pasha, was first performed in Cairo in December 1871). An essentially European city grew up between Ataba Square and the Nile, and the new Egyptian middle class spread northward. As Cynthia Myntti writes in *Paris Along the Nile: Architecture in Cairo from the Belle Époque* (1999), residents and visitors to Cairo could find "French and English bookshops, tea rooms and sidewalk cafés, fashionable boutiques, art galleries, and department stores. . . . Legendary hotels were built: Shepheard's, the Savoy, the Semiramis, and the Eden Palace. Later, cinemas and roller skating rinks were added for local amusement."

By the interwar years of the early twentieth century, after Egypt had been granted nominal sovereignty by the British and was ruled by a constitutional monarchy and parliamentary democracy in all matters except national security and control of the Suez Canal, Cairo became the most cosmopolitan city in the world. But six months before the 1952 revolution, on a day remembered as Black Saturday, anti-British mobs torched Cairo's

Western landmarks, including the Turf Club, major hotels, banks, cinemas, and residences. Ismail's Cairo was largely reduced to ashes, left smoldering under a thick pall of smoke. Nasser's Free Officers would hijack the popular unrest to seize power. When they did so six months later, they inherited not only the wealth and corruption of the former elite, but also the responsibility for rebuilding the capital city.

"Architecture is the art that so disposes and adorns the edifices raised by man . . . that the sight of them contributes to his mental health, power, and pleasure," wrote the nineteenth-century author, artist, and critic John Ruskin. No one would more strongly endorse that sentiment in Cairo these days than Samir A. Rafaat, a leading amateur historian and a descendant of an aristocratic family. Rafaat, an utterly charming man whose conversation reduces hours to minutes, has painstakingly documented the city's architectural past over the past few decades as it crumbled before his eyes. Much of his research was published in *Cairo, the Glory Years* (2003), which damns "the socialist state" under Nasser and his successors as the city's "new and useless landlord."

Given the present decay, overcrowding, and haphazard planning, he writes in the book's introduction, it may seem difficult to grasp that Cairo was once an architecturally attractive city. But the period from the end of the nineteenth century up until the 1950s "witnessed an architectural flowering that was unparalleled, with a variety of styles existing side by side: baroque, neo-classical, art nouveau, art deco, rococo khedival, colonial, Bauhaus, Italian Renaissance, arabesque, and neo-Pharaonic. Altogether this produced an eclectic riot of elegant buildings." Between 1960 and 1990, in contrast, "almost all of the construction east and west of the Nile could be written off as void of any architectural appeal." The new tenants of the once grand buildings "retreated into xenophobia. Their civic responsibilities did not get out of the front door." Under Al-Sadat in the 1970s a new policy of *infitah,* or economic "openness," was promoted. It further exacerbated the gap between the rich and the poor and produced a new army of overnight millionaires who helped form the second-tier rich: "high fee doctors, bankers, and lawyers whose principal job these days is to keep the new rich healthy, solvent, and out of jail." Like the Free Officers, they were men with no taste or vision or civic responsibility. They continue to flee the city for newfangled condominiums in self-contained, soulless compounds springing up on its outskirts, manifesting there in concrete a sort of urban Saudi Arabia of the mind. Meanwhile, the once grand downtown districts have been left to decay.

"All I see in the heart of the city is decline, decline, and more decline," Rafaat told me as we sipped cappuccinos at a trendy café in Zamalek, an up-market island in the heart of Cairo, once the center of old Egyptian money and European high-class society but now largely populated by the brats of the new "fat cats" with their flashy cars, superficially Westernized tastes, and awful English. They live in the bland apartment blocks where once stood beautiful villas.

The main post-coup problems came from a combination of government legislation and social changes, Rafaat told me, especially in the early 1960s when the crowning socialist law of rent control was introduced. "Supposedly everyone's lot could improve and there would be housing for all," he explained. "But few people's lot has improved, and there still isn't housing for all. The only clear result is the absolute and total deterioration of our architectural landscape: from the landmarks and way people live to maintenance and appreciation. Would you want to spend money on maintaining a building if you have an up-market villa that will bring in less than $100 a month in rent—the ceiling that was set in the 1950s and 1960s and is still enforced today? Take the Sidki building here in Zamalek, which has about forty apartments. Because of the rent controls, it brings in less than $200 a month. Can you seriously expect the owners to take proper care of it?"

In the prerevolutionary era, buildings were built in a healthy climate of social competitiveness, he explained, as each owner wanted to have a prime location and a distinctive façade that would serve to attract the kind of people who could both afford to live there and have the kind of taste that meant they would take pride in their new surroundings. "But in the socialist era, pride was thrown out of the window. All they wanted to do was house people like rats. Anything would do. We moved almost overnight from a period of eloquent and elaborate architecture to a period of impersonal architecture. You had a brain drain as well, exacerbating the situation. It included the architects, musicians, composers, writers . . . most of such people were muzzled across the board. If I'm an architect, and I suddenly find that the largest single employer is the public sector, which pays piecemeal, I'm going to look elsewhere. Our best architects simply transported themselves to the Gulf and other countries such as Libya."

All of this importantly coincided, according to Rafaat, with what was to be the last flood of the Nile, whose alluvial rhythms had been regulating Egyptian life since time immemorial and whose taming had a dramatic impact on the Egyptian psyche.

"It was like we thought in terms of B.F. and A.F.—Before the Flood and After the Flood," he said. "It regulated everybody's behavior. Then Nasser built the High Dam, and we cornered the Nile. It stopped in Aswan, and from there on became a canal. At the same time, we had new regulatory laws that started to govern our everyday lives. Supposedly free education meanwhile led eventually to no education. Free health care and social security led to no health care and no social security. In the midst of all this, creativity became a thing of the past. There's been an absolute downgrading in every aspect of all the things that could have led to the improvement and maintenance of a city like Cairo. What are we left with now? Well, what floats to the top at the end? It's the shit."

Only very recently have intellectuals like Rafaat publicly tried to come to terms with the decline, helped in part by the growing nostalgia for the prerevolutionary period.

"There is no longer fear of talking about the monarchy, about how Khedive Ismail did a lot for Egypt. But for so long these were taboo subjects," he said. "History for so long started and ended with 1952. Now we can address history more objectively, and there is a lot of revisionism going on. Historians are now much more professional than they could have been even until the early 1980s. Before then, we were writing to the rulers, and not to anybody else. Unfortunately, now it's too late to redress the situation. The damage has been done. All we can do is try to salvage the very little that is left."

Rafaat's father, Dr. Wahid Rafaat, was a French-educated constitutional lawyer and leading member of the Wafd Nationalist Party that briefly ruled in the 1920s, and which would be banned along with all other parties by the Free Officers after they seized power. Arrested after a bang on the door in the middle of the night and imprisoned by the Revolutionary Command Council on charges of high treason merely because he wrote a series of articles criticizing Nasser's foreign policies, Dr. Wahid was subsequently confined to years of house arrest. Later, when a position became available at the International Court of Justice, Egypt was the only Arab state to reject his otherwise unanimous nomination, thus spoiling his chances. If Rafaat's is therefore essentially a victim's narrative, it is nonetheless well worth listening to for the bird's-eye view his family commanded. Still, I asked the son that just as there had been a simplification of what the revolution was and what it achieved, was there not a danger now of glorifying the prerevolutionary era? Was it not a time when a tiny percentage of the population owned almost all of the wealth, when a feudal-like system left the majority of Egyptians in absolute poverty?

"It depends how you research it," he countered.

Of course, in Farouk's era there was a great deal of corruption, and nepotism was rampant. But Egypt was moving from being an occupied country, first by the Ottomans and then the British, toward independence. There was a great homegrown nationalist movement. There was a process of evolution under way. If left alone, the nationalists would have brought about much, much better results than the revolution—or so-called revolution—that interrupted the process of evolution. Even though Farouk's regime had its share of corruption, there was in parallel a sense and a feeling that things were evolving. The economy was improving. The institutions of civil society were in place. Given the laws of supply and demand, nationalists would have redressed the situation—however slowly. But that process was suddenly interrupted, and instead you had a brain drain. What is a country and its people without its cultural elite, without the institutions that produce such an elite? We suddenly had a new elite made up of officers who had nothing to offer but dogma and tunnel vision, who just couldn't see the whole picture. They thought they could redress the situation by using drastic methods. But now there was absolutely no accountability, and so even more corruption. Because your mayor was appointed, your councilman was appointed, your village head was appointed, you couldn't approach them after four years and say: Look, you are accountable to me and I will not vote you back into office. We had no say, the little man had no say.

The crumbling education system, for Rafaat, is now the root of all the problems. Nasser placed great pride in expanding it, boasting that a new school was being opened in Egypt almost every week. That was true. But what use are a million schools if there are sixty or more students in each class who are beaten by the teacher if they ask a dissenting question about even the least controversial of subjects, while the teachers themselves are paid less than the waiter in a local coffee shop, and all they do in class anyway is engage their charges in rote learning and propagate official government versions of history, religion, and politics? If all that sounds far-fetched, consider this: In 2006, Mubarak intervened personally in the case of an Egyptian student who failed her high school exams after criticizing the United States and her own government in an essay, ordering her papers to be re-marked so the student could be given a pass. The story of the young student was widely reported in the Arab media, and even debated in the Egyptian parliament. She was summoned and questioned by the authorities, reports said, over whether she was a member of a secret organization after it emerged that in her exam essay she accused Washington of backing corrupt dictators at the expense of the needs of their people. Dictators, of course, are fond of gesture politics, and Mubarak's quick action after news of the girl's plight was leaked to the media had the effect of distancing him from an embarrassing domestic scandal. But no amount of arbitrary presidential orders can mask the fact that when it comes to the Egyptian education system quantity has clearly come at the expense of quality, and that the consequences for the republic are much broader than the crude harassment of a poor student. As Rafaat told me,

The lack of education leads to a person's total loss of orientation, of a sense of where they come from and whatever cultural heritage they have. You stop identifying with that heritage because you don't have the mental capabilities to understand and appreciate it. Lack of education means that your history has become alien to you, and the end result is the city of Cairo that you see today. There are calls from time to time in the local media to preserve what heritage we still have, however much it's a case of too little too late. The truth is that we're already in lost time. We need a miracle. Anyway, the average Egyptian is so concerned with subsisting from day to day that everything else—his heritage, his beautiful door, his cleanliness, his role in the community—has become secondary to him.

Feeling somewhat depressed after listening to Rafaat's gloomy take on Egypt, it seemed appropriate that I should take up an offer to visit Ahmed Okasha—the president of the Egyptian Psychiatric Association, former president of the World Psychiatric Organization, and director of the World Health Organization's Center for Training and Research in Mental Health. A few days later, I drove out to meet this pioneer of psychiatry in the Arab world. He had recently opened a mental health resort on the road to Suez. From a distance, it looked like many of the five-star hotels that have mush-roomed off the desert road, but it spearheads the introduction of a new type of psychiatric health policy that aims to remove the social stigma that surrounds mental illness in Egypt. Set in a sprawling garden, it has a gym and multipurpose court, and a reception area with tall windows opening onto the garden, crucially letting in light from all directions to lift the spirit right on arrival.

The man who greeted me was a perfect advertisement for the aims of his facility. A rubicund figure in fine tailoring whose wide, beaming face was topped by a gorgeously coiffed shock of white hair, Okasha radiated well-being from every pore of his corpulent frame. As we took a tour of the facility, passing intermittently one of the several likenesses of the doctor in bronze and ink dotted around the hospital, I asked him whether he could shed light, too, on the mental condition of less fortunate Egyptians after five decades of brutal military dictatorship. He was only too willing to do so, it soon became apparent. He began by making what he said was a crucial distinction between mental health and the absence of mental illness.

"Health as defined by the WHO is the physical, social, and psychological well-being of the individual—not the mere absence of disease," he stated. "To be mentally healthy, there are four requirements to satisfy: the ability to adjust to the stresses of life, to balance between your abilities and expectations, to give and not only to take and be centered around others, and to be able to do something for your family and society." Over the past fifty years there had been a dramatic change in the psyche, he said, of what he (rather quaintly) repeatedly referred to as "the Egyptian" in the course of our conversation. "The Egyptian is historically known to have a very cynical and sarcastic sense of humor. If he can't find anyone to make fun of, he will make fun of himself. He is known to have a high degree of flexibility, and to be very region- and family-oriented. But he is very much against extremism, fundamentalism, and violence. His resilience is excellent. At the same time, all his motivations are altruistic—family-oriented, society-oriented, or religion-oriented."

But no longer, Okasha believes.

We don't see a lot of smiles when we walk in the streets, and there are many reasons for this. First of all, there is the poverty. Still more than 50 percent of Egyptians are poor—they live on less than two dollars a day. Then there is overcrowding, which has a tremendous effect on the personality of the individual. Cairo is the most overcrowded city in the world. Fifty-two thousand people live in every square kilometer. Nothing like this has happened anywhere else. Then there is the high unemployment, and the inability of young people to engage in free expression. Free expression gives you mental health and self-dignity. Democracy offers better mental health, but it has to be real democracy—which means transparency, accountability, and the ability to change the ruling authorities. . . . Egyptians now find there is no transparency in anything in their lives, and there is no accountability. None of the thieves who are ministers or other politicians are accountable to the poor people. We have had the same thing since 1952: The army rules the country.

Mubarak, he said, is trapped in this mental environment.

"He has been there for twenty-five years. And now he says, 'I am starting to implement reform!'" he said contemptuously. "Of course it's impossible, because reform is a mental schema. He is unable to do it. Instead, he tried to do certain things just to create an impression." More dangerous, Okasha insisted, is the creeping apathy that has taken hold of the Egyptian psyche. "When you expose people to so much mental torture, to so many stresses in life, they start to withdraw into a state of helplessness and hopelessness. This makes you indifferent: You don't care about a damn thing. I live in Egypt, they rule Egypt, but I have no relationship with them. Let me give you an example: Those who voted in the 2005 presidential election amounted to just twenty-two percent of the population. Even in Mauritania you get a turnout of seventy-two percent! And there is the electoral fraud here: The Egyptian High Court of Appeal found that ninety members elected to parliament in the latest elections are there because of fraud. This shows why Egyptians aren't bothered anymore who rules them."

Okasha concluded that this climate of fraudulence has also taken over religion. "Egyptians have reduced religion to rituals, including covering the head, praying, going on pilgrimage . . . but deep inside, the faith is not strong, because they lie and embezzle and behave unethically," he said, posing briefly next to a display of framed caricatures of himself published in the Egyptian newspapers over the decades.

> Yet Islam is a religion of peace, nonviolence, and mercy. What is the root of this? Since ancient times, the Egyptian has been known as a man who never leaves his place. His honor is his land. But after the 1952 revolution, and after all the economic crises, he was forced to leave, to go to Saudi Arabia and the Gulf in search of work. When you abandon a little of your honor, this affects your ethics. Before 1967, Nasser had given the Egyptian people some pride. But then the war turned out to be a fiasco, whatever they said at the time, and the people decided: We have no faith in what these people say, and so we'll go back to God. We'll think about the afterworld, because here there is no hope—although Islam tells you that you should enjoy life as if you were going to live forever, and you should behave as though you will die tomorrow.

Okasha does not share the pervasive nostalgia for the days before the revolution, considering it a dangerous delusion. "People who instead turn back to a past era, like that under King Farouk, were not alive at the time," he pointed out. "They think there was more free expression and more democracy. But let's not forget that 0.5 percent of everything in Egypt was owned by a certain class of people. There was free expression, and we certainly didn't have an emergency law. And it's true that the aesthetic appreciation of Egyptians has deteriorated tremendously since the revolution. But I'm very much against those who harp on the past, and I think it's completely wrong to compare the present to a distant past."

So what of the future? What are the chances that the present chaos and despair will somehow turn out to be constructive? Or should we abandon all hope of progress?

I would prefer to think that there will be some kind of constructive chaos. As long as the cognitive schemata of the present policy makers remain as they are now, I don't think we can progress and it will become mass chaos. But I can see from the mass media, the newspapers, from new intellectuals, that there is some hope that they will force the policy makers to change. My own belief is that as long as the policy leaders lack transparency, accountability, and change of authority, there will be chaos. Either there will be a coup d'état, or we will have Muslim extremism. Then again, there could be peaceful change brought about by political parties. We have to understand that the people in the National Democratic Party are Egyptians. When you sit with them, they speak as we are speaking now. But they can't act, because it is the armed forces who really rule, and if you speak out against them you get imprisoned. In any case, leadership means selecting the right people to help you do the job properly. Unfortunately, there is a triad of power, money, and authority. If you have one of these, you have the other two—and you don't want to give any of them up.

It was almost as if a wistful note had crept into his voice.

Like so many other regime initiatives, a longstanding family-planning campaign has yielded at best patchy results—much like ongoing attempts to end the near-universal practice of female genital mutilation in accordance with official fatwas declaring the practice un-Islamic, and eradicating mass illiteracy under a self-congratulatory national book-reading program led by the president's media-friendly wife, Suzanne. The 2006 national census revealed that an Egyptian is born every twenty-three seconds, pushing the total population, including those living abroad, to seventy-six million, an increase of 37 percent over the 1996 census figure. That means one in four Arabs is now an Egyptian. Cairo's present population alone is estimated at close to twenty million, compared to just half a million at the turn of the twentieth century; the latest census showed that the capital had the largest recent population growth (almost 11 percent) of all the country's governorates. The regime now predicts that by the year 2022 some 28 million people will be living in the capital city. Already it is home to 43 percent of the country's urban home-based population, 55 percent of all universities, 46 percent of all hospital beds, and 43 percent of all jobs—not to mention the army of unemployed, a million and a half Sudanese and Iraqi refugees, and a million Egyptians who must travel daily to the capital from outlying areas to resolve a personal matter in the Kafkaesque government bureaucracy. Cairo, it is clear, will continue to develop at breakneck speed—and along the lines of every urban planner's worst nightmare.

This chronic centralization can be directly traced to Nasser's paranoid authoritarianism. Working according to the philosophy that if you control the head you control the rest of the body, he made Cairo the absolute center of power, to the severe detriment of smaller cities and the Nile Delta and Upper Egypt (to the north and south of Cairo respectively). The Mediterranean coastal city of Alexandria, for example, the country's second largest city and Cairo's only historic rival to prominence, is these days a mere shadow of the city depicted in dozens of famous Egyptian movies dating back to the 1940s, where young men and women found love while vacationing. Popular songs from the era laud the city's cool sea breeze, the beauty of its women, and how easy love flourishes, while Lawrence Durrell's *Alexandria Quartet* paid nostalgic homage to the city's extraordinary cosmopolitanism as well as the seedy, sleazy, and endlessly fascinating stage it was then for the machinations of the great and not-so-great powers. Most of the city's famous expat-run restaurants and night spots are no longer in business, their owners long ago having returned to Europe for good. Only a few faded, elderly people remain from the once prosperous expatriate community of Greeks, Cypriots, Italians, French, and Armenians.

Instead, the fundamentalist Muslim Brotherhood has more lawmakers elected from Alexandria than from any other city. Where Durrell's Protestant and Orthodox-born heroes once held forth (at admittedly tedious length) about the mysteries of the cabbala and celebrated the beauty of their various mistresses, now the city's five million inhabitants have to be mostly content with memorizing the Qur'an. Gulf returnees apply their newly learned Wahhabi doctrine with a vengeance, insisting that their womenfolk bathe in the sea in a full *abeyya* and their children do not talk to Christian Egyptians because, since the latter are infidels, it is religiously forbidden for them to do so. Given this appalling social climate, the new Library of Alexandria, built at a cost of $230 million in an attempt to revive its fabled ancient predecessor (and resembling nothing so much as a giant satellite dish), has unsurprisingly failed to ignite a renaissance of scholarly acumen.

I was often reminded of Rafaat's description of Cairenes as being "housed like rats," and Okasha's tracing of the deterioration of the mental health of the impoverished Egyptian masses, when I visited the family of twenty-year-old Ehab, whom I had befriended on the train to Cairo from Upper Egypt during one of my frequent trips up and down the country. A tall, thin, and vulnerable-looking young man, he had been reading a newspaper in the train carriage I was traveling in. A young Egyptian reading anything is enough of an oddity to draw immediate attention; and I became more curious still when I noticed that he was reading the opinion (rather than the sports or crime) page. Later, we got chatting over a cigarette under the huge No Smoking sign in the baggage area between carriages. The prohibition was ignored not only by us, but also by the guard whose job it presumably was to enforce it. That all such bylaws—from littering to refusing to use taximeters or respect basic traffic regulations—are routinely ignored is symptomatic, of course, both of the failed system and the universal contempt Egyptians now have for authority, be it on the local or the national level.

Ehab, it turned out, was a student at a college in the southern city of Qena, about an hour from the tourist resort of Luxor. He was on his way home for a short break, and invited me to pay his family a visit in Cairo anytime I was free. Back in the 1990s, such sincerely meant invitations to dinner, even by ordinary Egyptians not working in the vast tourism industry, had been forthcoming on an almost hourly basis, but had since become few and far between. I initially put this down to the fact that in the intervening years I had become more intense, spoke Egyptian demotic fluently, and looked older and more worldly, and thus in sum was less approachable. However, on another train journey a professor at one of Cairo's universities had gently told me, after hearing me lament to my traveling companion the dwindling number of invitations, that if "people invite you it will cost them because it would be shameful to give you anything but the best food, and the problem these days is that they can't even afford to bring enough food to the table for their own children." At that time, mid-2007, food prices had risen 25 percent since just a year earlier, while wages were largely what they had been for a decade. This is part of a historic pattern. While the average wage is estimated to have increased by 60 percent between 1978 and 1988, for instance, prices increased during that decade by 300 percent, with particularly devastating results for the bulk of the population whose wages (unlike those of the superrich) had at best kept up with the official but widely disputed rate of inflation.

Ehab's family lived in a satellite city on the outskirts of Cairo called Medinat Al-Salam. Their ground-floor, three-room apartment was in a gray purpose-built concrete block identical to all the others surrounding it. The satellite city was built in the late 1970s as part of Al-Sadat's "open door policy," when the regime announced plans to build fourteen new city centers with the goal of redirecting urban growth toward the desert. It was launched with great fanfare, accompanied by lofty sentiments extolling the virtues of a dignified human habitat and a general improvement in the quality of life. Hard reality soon kicked in, though, as the regime predictably neglected its duty on the funding side, and the responsibility for development fell instead on the shoulders of private investors. The result was hit and miss. A number of the cities—including Medinat Nasr and 6th October—eventually flourished, both as residential and industrial centers, although neither concrete jungle has any redeeming architectural features. In the case of Medinat Nasr, success was largely due to the fact that it became a place of choice for high-ranking civil servants to set up home: The Egyptian regime, like all dictatorships, prioritizes taking care of its own. To this day the number of Egyptians who vote in elections for the ruling National Democratic Party (roughly seven million, according to the ever-unreliable official figures) is equal to the number of government employees, who are often bused to the polling stations as police line the surrounding streets to keep away supporters of opposition groups eager to cast their own votes. 6th October City has meanwhile become a base for the half million or so Iraqi refugees who have fled to Egypt in the wake of the U.S.-led occupation of their country in 2003 and the ensuing civil war.

The other satellite cities remain virtual ghost towns—an apt description for Medinat Al-Salam, whose inhabitants were originally lured by the government from the rooftops of downtown Cairo's once-grand apartment blocks, where they had been squatting for decades. In the last quarter of a century, it has seen virtually no major investments, private or otherwise, and still has the air of an upscale refugee camp, its inhabitants forever hoping to move somewhere else. Its remoteness adds to the overwhelming sense of gloom: I would visit Ehab's family on Friday mornings, the Muslim weekend, when Cairo's infamously congested streets are briefly free of traffic; but even then it would take almost an hour by taxi, and cost six dollars—the equivalent of three days' salary for a midlevel government employee.

That had been the occupation of Ehab's now-retired father, a proud patriarch who sat smoking quietly as he watched his nine children—five boys and four girls between the ages of four and thirty—jostle for space in the front room, where the television was blasting an old Egyptian movie above whose din Ehab's grandmother tried to tell me that she needed a new set of false teeth. Three beds substituted for sofas, so the living room could be transformed into a bedroom at night. "Have you finished reproducing yet, or are you trying to create an army?" I asked the father as the front door, which opened directly onto the grimy communal staircase, swung open again with a bang and yet more little children—cousins? nephews?—filed past me to ask the grandmother for a few cents to buy some candy. Ashraf, the eldest son, joked that he himself already had three kids, and was on a mission to reinforce the depleting family ranks. Or perhaps he was serious. In any case, the subject of getting married and having children, and then trying to make enough money to feed, clothe, and educate them, came to dominate our chats during my occasional visits, which continued whether Ehab was at college or at home. No one seemed to have time to think about, let alone the inclination to discuss, anything else, save for the occasional bitter aside that the president was "a son of sixty bitches."

The reason for this intense reality, which Dr. Okasha had adumbrated for me, was a case of simple math. Ehab's father received a monthly government pension of $75. A golden house rule was that each Friday the extended family would eat meat together, and two kilos cost $15. That left just $15 from the main monthly family income, slightly less than the monthly rent. In order to marry, Ashraf had filled a rented apartment with furniture bought on the hire-purchase (the Egyptian tradition is that the groom provides the apartment and furniture, the bride the electrical appliances), and his father had taken on the burden not only of paying for the deposit on the apartment but the $40 monthly installment repayments. Ashraf worked in the tourism industry for a monthly wage of $40, barely sufficient to pay his own rent and travel to and from work each day on public transport. Ehab's next eldest brother, Bassam, although trained as a lawyer, worked in a local café, because he could not afford the bribe needed to get a place in a local lawyers' firm. Anyway, he earned the same wage as a low-ranking lawyer ($2) for a twelve-hour workday, plus a dollar or so tips if he was lucky. But he would be paid only intermittently by the owner, who claimed the coffee shop did not make enough money for him to pay his staff on a regular basis. If that were not bad enough, Bassam was also responsible for settling the check of any customer who left without paying. A gently pious man who prayed five times a day, and in a permanent state of anxiety because the woman he wanted but could not afford to marry was being pursued by a wealthier rival, he told me he was facing a more immediate dilemma of whether or not to continue praying in the local mosque because many customers would wait for the call to prayer and then slip away while he performed his ablutions. There were days when he would have to pay about a dollar deficit in the cash till (a cup of tea or a water pipe sells for about twenty cents); after buying a sandwich for lunch and paying for public transport to and from work, he would therefore often find himself having spent more than he had earned. Ehab himself did not have to pay for college, because he had graduated in the top rank of his high school; but he still had to find $70 a year for text books, $12 for rent per month, occasional train travel to and from college, food, and utility bills (his clothes were castoffs from his older brothers). He said this money came from his father.

All of which begged the question: How on earth did the father manage to spend five times his monthly pension on his children? There were two avenues open, it turned out, to help keep the family's heads just above water. The first was a support system popular among neighbors, especially wives with small children, whereby each would pay a certain amount each month into a kitty and one would take the full amount each month on a rotating basis. The second was a constant round of begging from friends and extended family, especially if one of them had managed to secure employment in the Gulf (where even unskilled laborers can earn as much as a thousand dollars a month). Ehab was fortunate that his extended family placed a high value on education and, noticing early on that he was clever, had paid for him to take private lessons after school. Sending children to school without having arranged for a private tutor is, it is often said, like denying them notebooks or shoes. Egyptians now reportedly spend about $2.4 billion annually on private tutoring, helping to keep alive a vicious cycle whereby the teachers themselves are often too tired to teach effectively in class because they work as tutors until the early hours of the morning in order to supplement their measly two dollars-a-day income.

At least half of all Egyptian families are in the same boat as Ehab's.

Nasser's corrupt elite was in a prime position to exploit Al-Sadat's new economic openness in the 1970s. "New classes of people emerged alongside, and sometimes out of, the previously ascendant state bourgeoisie," writes James Jankowski in *Egypt: A Short History* (2000). "'Openers' engaged in import trade, in financial speculation, or serving as middlemen for foreign investors; 'suitcase merchants' peddling designer fashions or electronic fashions; a new layer of indigenous millionaires being chauffeured in Mercedes and residing in opulent villas near the pyramids." But for the bulk of Egyptians, like Ehab's family, things got much worse, their frustration deepened by the knowledge that those who did enjoy a new-found prosperity in the 1970s rarely came by it honestly. Commissions and kickbacks became a normal part of doing business across the board. Higher officials took payoffs when they were not busy embezzling the state coffers, property developers cut every corner they could, and bureaucrats collected baksheesh just to perform their administrative duties. It is difficult to underestimate the impact on social status, in addition to class, of all this "bad money" replacing "good money." Just as Nasser's band of thugs and ignoramuses had replaced the old sophisticated aristocracy and cultural elite, now their own ranks were being swelled by those members of the nouveau riche who had attained their wealth suddenly merely by taking those kickbacks, traveling to the Gulf to work in the wake of the 1970s oil boom, or selling land that had been in their impoverished families for generations but had overnight come to be worth a small fortune as the property market catering to the new elite boomed. Rafaat's laconic summary of "shit rising to the top" again comes to mind.

When economic liberalization came in the form of privatization, it carried a heavy social price on those who had been left behind. Direct state subsidies for basic consumer goods were cut at the insistence of the World Trade Organization and International Monetary Fund, and about four hundred of Egypt's main public-sector companies have been privatized since the 1990s. Top officials are routinely accused of taking enormous kickbacks on the deals, and the newly established private companies therefore subsequently remain largely free of serious governmental regulation. One example of what happens when a corrupt government and ruthless private investors are joined at the hip is the phenomenon in Egypt of electricity and telecommunications towers being built next to, or on occasion even on top of or inside, the houses of the poor, who are told when they complain to officials that there are no laws restricting such practices and so their children—already suffering from malnutrition and lack of health care—will just have to live with the fact that they are potentially being permanently exposed to high levels of cancer-causing radiation. In tandem with this selfishness and neglect, the regime continues to increase dramatically spending on the military, while cutting spending on social services such as education and health care. This is all in line with the new global orthodoxy, where wealth created by the free market is supposed to trickle down and thus benefit all, with no requirement therefore to put in place alternative mechanisms of social support.

It would be easy to find a family in similar dire straits in any of the many quasi slums of London or New York, with the same complaints about substandard housing, health care, and education, not to mention government corruption and indifference. What makes Britain and the United States different, though, is the reality of social mobility, and along with it the important self-knowledge that, whatever one's background, a good education and a willingness to work hard may eventually find appreciation and so propel one out of the cycle of poverty and despair. In short, there exists a middle class. While it is true that people in neglected public housing in Britain and the United States may also remain pretty much stuck in the cycle of poverty for the rest of their lives, and the gap between the haves and have-nots also continues to widen in these and other developed countries, the middle class is, in contrast to Egypt, an economically more significant demographic because they are paid comparatively more. Moreover, and likewise in contrast to Egypt, there is some form of democratic governance, and so the concerns of the masses must at least be listened to, if not always acted on. In Egypt, the nominal middle class, which Ehab's brother Bassam as a trained lawyer should long since have joined, has been feeling the sharp end of a succession of economic reforms undertaken by the regimes since Nasser's death in 1970, while political stagnation has helped cement that gap and marginalize the middle class's role in helping to shape politics and society. The Egyptian regime likes to boast that the economy has been enjoying its highest growth rates since the revolution. But seven hundred thousand Egyptians enter the job market every year, and the public sector still employs roughly seven million citizens whose jobs cannot be privatized, however overburdened the state bureaucracy. A question often asked is: How many of the seventy-eight million Egyptians benefit from the Cairo and Alexandria stock exchange?

The general conclusion to draw is perhaps the most obvious, namely, that impoverishing, and thereby eviscerating, the middle class is bad for any country's long-term stability. This is doubly so when the patron state washes its hands of both management of the economy and social welfare, leaving the tens of millions of the underclass likewise adrift in the resulting uncertain currents. One danger is that the vacuum will provide the perfect environment for the growth of an organization like the Muslim Brotherhood, whose rank-and-file members are primarily made up of what is left of the educated middle class: doctors, engineers, lawyers, students, teachers. The organization has made grassroots charity and an ostensible concern for the suffering of the downtrodden the central prong in its campaign to win over the masses to hard-line Islam.

If the Brotherhood attains power, its rule may decades hence prompt in some Egyptians a nostalgia for the last days of the present corrupt military regime that Egyptians now feel for the parliamentary democracy that existed before the coup in 1952.

CHAPTER TWO

THE BROTHERS

The Muslim Brotherhood recently built an eight-story building in a Cairo suburb to serve as the headquarters for their new parliamentary deputies. Despite being flush with cash from charitable donations and adrift in Egypt's tumultuous political seascape of corruption and nepotism, they are rarely profligate, and in this instance they could make a convincing case that it was money wisely spent. In the 2000 elections they had won just fifteen of the four hundred and fifty-four seats up for grabs, but now that they had taken eighty-eight in the December 2005 polls, they needed extra office space. In consolidating their presence in the five-year legislative assembly, the Muslim Brotherhood also cemented their reputation, at home and abroad, as the largest, best-organized, and most disciplined opposition force in Egypt. But despite their higher profile, what they stand for exactly remains confusing, not only to the West but also to many Egyptians. Founded in 1928 by Hassan Al-Banna as a protest movement against corrupting Western cultural influence and British political control of Egypt under the oversight of a decadent puppet monarchy, the Muslim Brotherhood remains primarily dedicated to bringing Egyptians into the tight grip of a strict interpretation of Islam. The group's secondary aim is to reassess Egypt's dependent political and military alliance with the United States, especially—but not exclusively—with regard to the Palestinian question. And in a distant future, they envisage the reestablishment of an Islamic caliphate based on a romanticized notion of what life was like under the Rightly Guided Caliphs following the death of the Prophet.

Al-Banna's original motivation, as one historian has put it, was the "reform of hearts and minds, to guide Muslims back to the true religion, and away from the corrupt aspirations and conduct created by European dominance." In battles against Israel after the Jewish state's creation in 1948, and against British occupation soldiers along the Suez Canal in the early 1950s, the group's paramilitary wing (which no longer exists) distinguished itself as fearless and dedicated. It even won admiration among Egyptian nationalists who otherwise had no time for the group's hardline Islamist agenda. But in 1954 the organization was banned, then almost annihilated by Nasser. He claimed they tried to assassinate him while he delivered a public speech in October that year in Alexandria, the shots heard live on Egyptian radio. The Brothers denied any involvement in the events of that day. Nasser, it should be noted, was not beyond conjuring up such spectacular crises to shore up his domestic support—having likely arranged, for instance, the bombing of the landmark coffee shop Groppi's in the heart of downtown Cairo in a bid to create instability at the height of his power struggle with the first figurehead leader of the republic.

In any case, by that time the Muslim Brotherhood had hundreds of thousands of followers, who would remain stubbornly loyal to their vision of an Islamic state however many of their comrades were hanged or sentenced without trial to hard labor or tortured to death by Nasser's thugs. A whole generation of Brothers came to be radicalized by the torture, prison camps, and executions. This was especially true of those who came under the spell of Sayyid Qutb, a Brother who was executed in August 1966 (along with a number of other leaders) after a false charge of conspiracy was brought against them. In his books, which were the real reason Nasser had him hanged, Qutb argued that the Nasserist state belongs to the Islamic category of *jahiliyya,* or "pre-Islamic ignorance"—a designation that, for him, placed the regime beyond the bounds of Islam, and therefore justified its violent overthrow. From the early 1970s until the late 1990s, the military establishment would face down a wave of Islamist terror, inspired in part by Qutb's writing, and carried out by jihadist groups who had split from the Muslim Brotherhood after accusing the leadership of being too accepting of the status quo and military regime. The violence during those three decades included the assassination of Al-Sadat in 1981, the murder of secular intellectuals, and frequent attacks on the minority Christian community, culminating in the massacre of dozens of tourists near the resort town of Luxor in Upper Egypt in 1997.

In contrast, the Muslim Brotherhood renounced violence in the early 1970s, cautiously embraced the democratic process, and publicly distanced themselves from Qutb's more radical agenda. Under the spiritual guidance of moderate Omar Al-Tilimsani especially, the new Muslim Brotherhood emerged as a key contributor to the debate about Egyptian identity in the wake of Egypt's humiliation in the 1967 war and Nasser's death three years later. The debate was centered on the future, but revolved around a question of the past: Should Egyptian history be interpreted along nationalist, Arabist, Islamist, ethnic, or pro-Western lines—or a combination of all these?

Since the time of Mohammed Ali, Cairo has been pulled between the hedonism of Paris to the West and the austerity of Mecca to the East. While the nationalists, progressive Islamists, and cultural elite fighting foreign occupation—Christian and Muslim—could embrace the best the West had to offer in their drive for Egyptian independence, the Muslim Brotherhood cast Mohammed Ali and his heirs, especially Khedive Ismail, as decadent squanderers of the country's wealth and opportunistic transgressors of Islamic norms and values whose behavior encouraged among the masses by example a disregard for Islam. For the more radical Islamists, this was the root cause of the country's decline, and it was reversing the trend rather than embracing Western-style democracy that, they believed, provided the key to the country's salvation, returning Egypt and its people to its natural sphere of Islamic inspiration and influence.

In *Egypt's Belle Époque*, Trevor Mostyn documents the dark underbelly of nineteenth-century Egyptian life often overshadowed by the more familiar stories of world-class exhibitions, glittering parties, and sumptuous palaces, which led to popular resentment that both Islamists and nationalists, notwithstanding their different agendas, would tap into. Rather than being championed as an accidental harbinger of progressive, modernizing change, Napoleon and his occupation army were seen in retrospect by the Muslim Brotherhood as little more than crude Islamophobic vandals. They had plenty of ammunition, as Napoleon's avowed respect for Islam mattered little in practical terms when, having torn down the barricades of Egyptian mobs protesting the French occupation, the French under his command rode into the mosque of Al-Azhar, the preeminent Islamic institution of learning, tethered their horses to the prayer niches, trampled on Qur'ans, and for good measure urinated on the mosque floor. After getting drunk on wine, they proceeded to strip Muslim worshippers caught in the middle of this chaos and stole their possessions.

Similarly, Ismail's decision to refashion Cairo on the Parisian model in preparation for the celebrations surrounding the opening of the Suez Canal in 1869 may have impressed his European guests and his own pampered circle; but the downside was that it bankrupted the Egyptian treasury, leading to his being deposed and the British occupying Egypt in all but name. When the British and French consuls ordered Ismail to abdicate, Mostyn writes, he "could not call on his people because his taxes and tyranny had made him hated by them." Stories of Ismail's sexual promiscuity abounded, not to mention the possible murder of various unfaithful mistresses; even liberal-minded Egyptians who were unconcerned with their ruler's private life, but who considered themselves equal to the British and French, bristled at the latter's special treatment as guests of the khedive. Their own exclusion from the upper-class lifestyle of the new European quarters of Cairo, from which all but the best-connected and most Westernized Egyptians were banned, was a continuous source of humiliation.

Not, of course, that Cairo's underclass had anything to sing and dance about, either. Mostyn quotes a description of their suffering from Lucie Duff Gordon's *Letters from Egypt* a year after the Suez Canal celebrations took place, which begins: "I cannot describe to you the misery here now." Every day, she continues, there is "some new tax. Now every beast, camel, cow, sheep, donkey, horse is made to pay. The *fellaheen* can no longer eat bread; they are now living on barley-meal mixed with water and raw green stuff, vetches, etc." The contemporary poet Salih Magdi expressed the collective disgust of the Egyptian masses at the rule of the elite, and especially Ismail himself:

Your money is squandered on pimps and prostitutes.
Normal men take a woman for a wife;
He wants a million wives.
Normal men take a house for a living;
He takes ninety.
Oh Egyptians, there is disgrace all around:
Awake, Awake!

By the time of King Farouk's reign, the gap between the rich and the poor had grown wider still. "Poor peasants could not afford tuition payments to send their sons and daughters to school; indeed they could not do without even the meager incomes they gained from their children's work in the fields," writes Arthur Goldschmidt in *Modern Egypt: The Formation of a Nation State* (2004). Mortality rates, especially for babies and children in rural areas, Goldschmidt adds, were among the world's highest. The poorest lacked even houses; vagabonds slept in doorways, under bridges, and on railroad rights-of-way.

If this sounds like the Egypt of today, it is because the parallels are indeed strikingly relevant. They serve as a reminder, too, that Egypt has come full circle; they serve as a reminder that the nostalgia for the Farouk era in some sections of the contemporary elite is partly symptomatic of an idealized remembrance of things past that overlooks the reality that most Egyptians of the time confronted in their daily lives. With one crucial difference: In the etiolated Egypt of today, the excesses of the ruling class produce nothing at all of value. Corruption under Farouk was a rich, festering, cosmopolitan seedbed of indigenous art and culture, subsuming imported notions from here, there, and everywhere in a special "Egyptianness" that was defined precisely by its hybrid nature; unjust, yes, in its own way as violent and cruel as the present, but varied, untidy, and fertile enough to accommodate a multitude of individual aspirations—even if those aspirations were as likely as not to remain unfulfilled. It offered, in a word, hope. In the all but ethnically cleansed and culturally purged post-Nasser Egypt, by contrast, even money has gone stale, producing for the rich only a barren imitation of life elsewhere, and financing only the thugs' indulgence in beating any individual expression to a pulp.

Anwar Al-Sadat liked to promote an image of himself as a pious man of the people, even as he sold Egypt's soul to a West that fascinated him and by which he longed to be embraced and respected. Even before the 1952 military coup, he had cultivated ties with Muslim Brotherhood leaders. As the new president moving to sideline Nasser's clique in order to replace it with his own in the early 1970s, he quickly brought the Brothers back into the mainstream, and his encouragement of Islamist youth movements facilitated especially the birth of what would become powerful Muslim student associations in the republic's universities. "I want to raise Muslim boys, and to spend money on them, because they will be our anchor," he explained. The Brothers are enthusiastic about private ownership—an Islamic principle and not at all Communist—so they initially embraced Al-Sadat's *infitah* policies that appeared to open up economic space for individual initiative and reward, a promise of change from the Nasser period during which only conformity with the regime was compensated and opposition punished. However, their increasingly bold criticism of the corruption and class divisions that privatization helped exacerbate and the signing of the peace treaty between Egypt and Israel once again opened the gap between them and the military regime. Following Al-Sadat's assassination in 1981 by yet more radical Islamist extremists enraged by his visit to

Israel, Mubarak, despite initial moves at rapprochement, redesignated the Muslim Brotherhood hotheaded outlaws. The emergency law reenacted following Al-Sadat's assassination meant they could be arrested at any time and for any reason, at the whim of the regime. One of the many consequences still being played out are the hundreds of Islamists once again shackled in Egypt's torture chambers. It has to be said categorically that members of the Muslim Brotherhood, especially grassroots members who joined from deep conviction, have suffered, and suffered atrociously and often with great fortitude, at the hands of the regime. For their leaders, that reality has offered an opportunity for a not entirely unearned self-portrayal as martyrs to the causes of freedom and justice.

Under the emergency law, those from among the Muslim Brotherhood ranks who stand in elections must still do so officially as "independent" candidates. They openly campaign, though, under the most famous of their array of simplistic party slogans—"Islam Is the Solution"—so everyone knows their real affiliation; and in the ground-floor reception of their new headquarters, where I had come to meet the head of the movement's parliamentary bloc, I was greeted with a poster announcing their more militant credo: "The Koran is our constitution. The Prophet is our leader. Jihad is our way. Death for the sake of God is our highest aspiration."

A few months after the December 2005 elections took place, I met with prominent Muslim Brotherhood deputy Hamdy Hassan at the new party headquarters in Cairo. Hassan is also the spokesman for the parliamentary opposition bloc. He is a tall, middle-aged, balding man, who dresses (like all Muslim Brotherhood officials) smartly in a suit and tie. He offered a firm handshake and broad smile as I slipped off my shoes. We made our way, over prayer mats, to settle down on a sofa. Why, I wondered, are we meeting in a prayer hall, when there were eight floors in this new headquarters? Hassan, I was to discover, embodied everything that critics of the Muslim Brotherhood find infuriating about the organization: a tendency to deal in abstractions rather than specifics, reduce arguments to slogans, and tell outsiders what he thinks their governments want to hear. He ruffled my feathers at the outset by insisting on speaking formal Arabic, despite my protestation that I spoke the Egyptian dialect and so would find it more difficult to follow what he was saying this way. Many Islamists prefer to orate in the more formal version of their language, which is derived from the Qur'an, as they view it as relatively uncorrupted by contemporary trends and fashions—the vulgar—and therefore closer to the language spoken by the Prophet. But almost no other Egyptian is able to speak it fluently, nor do they enjoy listening to others speak it. In fact, they are proud of how their dialect has become the lingua franca of the Arab world, largely because of the historic regional dominance of Cairo's television, movie, and music industries. It is bizarre that a group claiming to represent the true interest of Egyptians, and that makes so much of its social programs, maintains such a fundamental disconnect from the common Egyptian. In the end, rather oddly, we relied on the services of a translator—from Hassan's highbrow formal to my English or more quotidian Arabic dialect. Perhaps his intransigence offered a glimpse of how dogma may triumph over the sensible and the practical, should Hassan and his colleagues one day attain political power.

Since the December 2005 elections, Hassan told me, he had twice been arrested. "Family and even friends and associates of other Muslim Brotherhood members are routinely arrested or harassed. The regime's aim is to intimidate us into giving up on our efforts to achieve our religious and political objectives." But they would not be diverted from their course any more than be forced into an irrational response in the form of directly challenging the regime or resorting to violence. Sudden revolutionary change, he was eager to make clear, is anathema to everything he and his colleagues stand for. "If there were sudden change in Egypt, there would be chaos, and that would be bad for both Egypt and the rest of the world," he explained.

What, I wanted to know, had his personal platform been as a candidate in the election, to provoke such wrath by the state? He answered:

> This is my second term as a deputy, and my philosophy is that the human being is a part of his society. The Muslim Brotherhood are in all places in society, in NGOs and local governments and syndicates. This makes our program different from all the others. We look at the economic and educational and social aspects of the country's problems. We are answering the needs of the people in all of the country's governorates on each and every level. And we target ordinary people in the streets to find out what their needs are and then try to satisfy them. We do not want an Islamic republic, but a modern civilization; but it will have an Islamic foundation. We have no problem with democracy or a constitution. We have no problem with the mechanism of a modern civilization. We are a powerful opposition in parliament, and we can make our voices heard.

His answer left me none the wiser, certainly not about what he and others had done to be harassed, arrested, and jailed. After all, nothing in what he said was objectionable or threatening. A liberal might wonder whether holding that a human being is a part of his society might mean that individual rights are subordinate to the common good, defined by whom being unclear. But the regime is hardly liberal. Perhaps the regime is more concerned about the Muslim Brotherhood seeking to answer the needs of the people, implicitly indicting the regime for its incompetence.

But rather than pursuing the philosophical, I turned to the pragmatic, asking instead about the unofficial coalition the Muslim Brotherhood had formed with socialist and other opposition deputies in parliament, and with grassroots pro-democracy groups like Kifaya (Enough) that had been leading demonstrations against the Mubarak regime in the streets. Could Islamists and secularists forge a common agenda in the name of the Egyptian people?

"Many things make us stand together, especially political issues like whether Gamal Mubarak will become president," he replied. "We are all against that. We also all favor political reform, freedom of political parties, the ending of the emergency law, and freedom of the press. Our common ground is in the political sphere."

What about freedom of expression? If the Qur'an is to be the constitution, would that not impose restrictions on Egyptian society that the secularists would resist?

"In an Islamic country there is complete freedom of expression for all the people," Hassan said matter-of-factly. "Islamic history emphasizes this point very clearly. In the past, every citizen had the right to speak to the leader of the Muslim community or nation whenever they liked: men and women, citizens and noncitizens, Muslims and non-Muslims. An Islamic state does not differentiate between these people. This is the basis of our religion, and not a question of politics. This would be part of our constitution, because the Qur'an is our constitution. Why do we make people slaves when they are born free?"

I asked what the relationship of this Brotherhood-led state would be with the United States.

"America should not fear the Muslim Brotherhood," he said. "America is calling for greater freedom and democracy. They say they invaded Iraq and toppled Saddam Hussein in the name of democracy. The reality is the opposite. They support the Arab dictators who oppress their people with steel and fire, and deny them democracy and human rights. There is torture in our prisons, as has been made clear by the publication of lots of photographs and other evidence."

Indeed. But so far his answer provided little optimism for positive relations; after all, he in effect called the United States hypocritical and responsible for the suffering of the Arab people. How about, I said, answering my question: What would be the relationship between the Brothers and the United States?

"This is our homeland, and we belong to this land," he mumbled. "So why does the United States come and tell us what to do through its dictators? We should train ourselves to better ourselves, and be a country both democratic and Islamic, and also respectful of Western traditions. Why don't we get to enjoy the vast treasures of our country? Why don't we get to live in safety and dignity?"

Getting a straight answer from Hassan was proving harder work than getting blood from a stone. But it was perhaps worth asking one more question. Many people, I put to him, argue that the Muslim Brotherhood helps Mubarak, because they give him a trump card in his dealings with Washington. The Americans are so afraid of Islamic movements that Mubarak is able to brush off criticism with reference to the Muslim Brotherhood while continuing to rely on massive amounts of financial aid that serves as the foundation of his regime's patronage. Does this reality not make him feel uncomfortable?

"The reigning regime is using us to frighten the United States," he quickly concurred, then sank into silence. I pressed him: How do you feel about this contradiction? "What exactly is the contradiction?" he asked in turn, confused. I repeated the question more clearly. "The years of Mubarak's rule are just a few drops in the ocean of the life of this nation," he declared solemnly. "For example, the Soviet Union was just seventy years old when it started to collapse. We know that the future is for us. We will be friends of any country that wants to be friends with us. We have faith, and we know we are justified in what we call for. I think that any Western country that truly understands us would be on our side, and not on the other side, against us. This is because we have principles that are applicable to all places and for all the people in the world. They would bring peace and security throughout the world, and with it justice and equality for all. There would not be any wars or famines if our principles were applied."

He did not care what the U.S. government says or does against the Muslim Brotherhood, he concluded. "We know that there is no problem between our philosophy and the beliefs of the Western people," he insisted. "The problem is only with the leaders. They seem to have something bad in their heart that is both against our people and ourselves."

Middle East historian Elie Kedourie wrote in his classic essay "The Middle East and the Powers": "One of the simplest and yet most effective means known to mankind of keeping in touch with reality is to contrast what people say with what they do, to compare professions with performance." He was talking about how the West can often misrepresent the Arab world due to remoteness and a lack of familiarity, but such an approach is also useful on the ground when analyzing the goals of the Muslim Brotherhood—and Hamdy Hassan in particular.

In the 2000–2005 parliament, Muslim Brotherhood MPs focused most of their attention on restricting free expression in the three key arenas of culture, media, and education, control that is essential to their agenda of Islamizing society from the grass roots. One is tempted to give them grudging respect for their strategy. By combining general references to Islamic values that tap into deep-rooted morals, a vague agenda that is open to interpretation and elicits the sympathies of divergent groups, and a practical agenda that focuses on culture, they are playing an adroit game of competing for the hearts and minds of various constituencies. Their ferocious attack on Culture Minister Farouk Hosni when he called the wearing of the veil a sign of backwardness was further proof of an ongoing cultural offensive. After all, if a woman wants to protect her honor and abide by Islamic tradition, then should she not have the right to do so? Calling wearing the veil backward simply added insult to injury by disparaging rather than respecting both the individuals and the tradition. But the right of expression only goes so far with the Muslim Brotherhood. *Al-Ahram* noted that *The Brothers in the 2000–05 Parliament,* a book that details the performance of the group's fifteen deputies in that period, cites former Brotherhood MP Gamal Heshmat as taking the credit for previously forcing Hosni to ban the publication of three novels that the Brotherhood said promoted blasphemy and unacceptable sexual practices. According to *Al-Ahram Weekly,* the book also revealed that Hamdy Hassan himself has consistently been at the forefront of the Muslim Brotherhood's campaign to kill off cultural expression, from literature to beauty contests, with accusations of blasphemy as his bullets. He holds Hosni personally responsible for taking the lead in "the current US-led war against Islamic culture and identity," the book stated, and it revealed, too, that of the total number of questions asked by Brotherhood MPs in the 2000–2005 session 80 percent were on cultural or media issues.

Not that any of this should come as a surprise. Culture is a powerful force, especially in a society where it is largely controlled by the state. By controlling culture, the state acts paternalistically, and, like any father figure, its own actions, and nonactions, are seen as indicative of fitness to exercise authority. The Muslim Brotherhood clearly understand that values and morals resonate emotionally with the people, and use deviation and deviance as a tool of reproach. And here Hassan's argument that "the human being is part of his society," if followed to its conclusion, could perhaps take on a rather ominous coloring: Since society is more important than the individual, then the individual must either conform or be excluded lest his or her deviation spread. As Barry Rubin details in *Islamic Fundamentalism in Egyptian Politics* (2002), since the early 1990s "moderate" Islamist groups like the Muslim Brotherhood have used intimidation to control Egypt's social and intellectual life, a struggle that has utilized "legal actions, teaching, non-governmental organizations meeting citizens' needs, and lobbying activities." Of the many incidents and battles, the case that drew the widest international attention was that of Professor Nasir Hamid Abu Zayid of Cairo University, accused by one of his pious colleagues of blasphemy for a 1992 book that used critical scholarly methods to analyze phrases in the Qur'an. After a series of conflicting decisions in lower courts, a Cairo court ruled that Zayid was indeed an apostate from Islam, about the worst form of deviation within sharia and punishable by death. Indeed, some clerics called on the government to execute him. The judgment of the court, however, was limited to the immediate issue at hand: whether Zayid's wife, as a good Muslim woman in need of protection, should be forcibly divorced from him; that is, regardless of her own wishes, should the state intervene to protect her good name and honor. And this the court decided was just, ordering such a separation. The couple fled to Europe, where they remain in exile. It is difficult to believe that, should the Muslim Brotherhood take control of parliament, they would invite them back. Indeed, the Islamist lawyer who brought the case against Zayid, as an individual, not as a member of the Muslim Brotherhood, was euphoric. "This is just the beginning," Rubin quotes him as saying. "We will do this to anyone who thinks they are bigger than Islam."

Of course, the Islamists' perpetual argument that their agenda not only embraces democracy but in fact takes it to a higher level of true popular participation is eyewash. Western democracies in theory guarantee the political participation of all citizens regardless of ideology, opinion, or religion; but the Muslim Brotherhood and their like make political participation of individuals in society subject to the principles of the sharia—no one, after all, is "bigger than Islam." In the West, the legislative and judicial branches of government monitor state actions to ensure they conform to democratic rules: The three powers keep each other in check. In an Islamist setup, the actions of the state would be monitored by the Muslim Brotherhood to ensure they conform to the rules of sharia. In other words, the Islamists would monitor only themselves. The Muslim Brotherhood guarantees freedom of belief only for the followers of the three revealed (Abrahamic) religions, since the Qur'an, due to the Prophet's particular circumstances, is wholly ignorant of, say, Buddhism, and only takes issue with polytheism (of which Mecca was a center in his time), which it naturally condemns since it seeks to supersede it. And the freedom of association enjoyed by civil organizations in a democracy would, in an Islamist system, be conditional on their adherence to the strictures of the sharia. The Brotherhood opposes the notion of a state based exclusively on Western-style democratic institutions: Islamic government is based on the *shura* (consultative assembly) system, veneration of the leader, and the investiture of a Supreme Guide. So, says the Islamic canon, and it must therefore be. In short, it is a circular argument, positing that perfect freedom and human rights have already been achieved in the Islamist democracy, obviating the need for any doubt, debate, expression, exploration, and whatever else fuels the development of a culture, except for such minor niggles as the ruler may from time to time bend his august ear to. That is the principle guiding Saudi Arabia, and the results are there for all to see in the arid kingdom's magnificent achievements over the last seven decades in music, art, literature, philosophy, science, and technology.

When the Muslim Brotherhood laid down its first detailed political platform in October 2007, it showed its true colors. Women and Christians would be barred from becoming president, and a board of Muslim clerics would oversee the government in a move that many observers noted was terrifyingly reminiscent of Iran's Islamic state. The president cannot be a woman because the post's religious and military duties "conflict with her nature, social and other humanitarian roles," the document said. Amazingly, the blueprint reportedly discussed women's issues under its "Issues and Problems" chapter, alongside other "problems" like unemployment and child labor. While underlining "equality between men and women in terms of their human dignity," it warned against "burdening women with duties against their nature or role in the family."

The election of so many Islamist deputies in 2005 was the culmination of a long journey by the Muslim Brotherhood, punctuated by constant battles against the despotic tools of persecution, torture, and execution. For many observers, it was also another important marker in the group's evolution away from violence. The Muslim Brotherhood's gradual move into mainstream Egyptian politics is being watched closely in the West, as other Islamist political parties that are almost all offshoots of the Muslim Brotherhood experiment with elections and democracy throughout the Arab and wider Islamic world. Muslim Brotherhood activities vary from country to country, and the chapters are officially independent; but leaders in Egypt have been quoted as saying that they are all united in their beliefs and take advice from the main Egyptian chapter. Their strong showing in the Egyptian elections has triggered a flood of papers in policy journals by Middle East analysts. Most call for Washington's greater engagement with the group, which is increasingly viewed in realist foreign policy circles as the lesser of the two evils, when compared to the military regime, in the domestic Egyptian political scene.

However, perhaps what looked on the surface like an electoral triumph for the Brothers was anything but. They won 20 percent of the seats; but at most 25 percent of Egyptians voted. And since the latter figure was provided by the regime, even that should be viewed with extreme skepticism. Anyone who strolled the streets of Egypt on parliamentary election day would have found it difficult to find a local who even knew the election was taking place, let alone one who had any knowledge about their local candidates or was actually making his or her own way to the polling station. But even accepting the official turnout figures, the Muslim Brotherhood could only muster the support, according to one interpretation of the results, of a small minority of the voting-age population, despite opinion polls indicating that the overwhelming majority is deeply dissatisfied with the regime's performance. Implicitly, this argument posits that the 25 percent who turned out were a sample representative of the whole. But there is no concrete reason to believe this, either. There are two implications. One is that those who did turn out were motivated, that the Muslim Brotherhood was particularly motivated, and thus the 20 percent is an overestimate. Conversely, the Muslim Brotherhood supporters may not have turned out much due to fear, so the results could be an underestimate. The point is that we have no way of knowing, even assuming that the reported figures are legitimate and not manipulated by the government—down or up, the latter to strike fear in the West. The bottom line is that to call the results a triumph for the Muslim Brotherhood is a very rash conclusion.

In addition to these complicating (and in the West, largely ignored) details is plenty of anecdotal evidence suggesting that many—perhaps the majority—of those who vote for the Islamists do so not because they have any great love for what they stand for, notwithstanding their own "turning inward" and becoming more privately religious in the wake of the 1967 defeat, but in protest at the corruption and brutality of a military regime that has succeeded in crushing all secular alternatives. This has echoes of the Hamas story in the Occupied Territories, and we all know how that has ended up. The story of the Muslim Brotherhood, this alternative narrative suggests, is not so much one of triumph in the face of adversity as a failure to garner mass popular support despite a social, political, and economic malaise in Egypt that elsewhere has proved a hugely fertile environment for the spread of Islamism—radical or otherwise.

The widely accepted argument that the Egyptian state was deeply unnerved by the Muslim Brotherhood's unexpected success at the 2005 polls—as evidenced by widespread fraud, violent attacks by riot police against Muslim Brotherhood supporters in the streets, and physical assaults on individuals in Muslim Brotherhood strongholds in an attempt to stop them from casting their votes—should also be looked at more critically. After the polls closed, the security forces did resume their arbitrary arrests of Muslim Brotherhood members, partly in an attempt by the regime to keep the new parliamentary deputies in line; and the regime did then decide to postpone scheduled local council elections in apparent fear of yet more Muslim Brotherhood gains. On the surface, this gives the impression of a regime resentful and afraid of the sudden rise of the Brothers, if not of outright paranoia. But it should always be remembered that in Egypt it is, according to Mubarak's critics, the military regime, and its representative president, who ultimately decide the winners and losers in elections, both parliamentary and presidential; and, for that matter, by what margin. Context, then, is all. The 2005 elections occurred at a rather curious time. The Americans were once again on a democracy kick, at least in public, which was inconsistent with their support for authoritarian regimes like Mubarak's—as the Muslim Brotherhood never tires of pointing out. In the lead-up to the 2005 elections, then, Mubarak was under limited pressure for a brief period from Washington to fast-track a permanently delayed domestic reform program. Would it stretch imagination too much if Mubarak's regime viewed a larger Muslim Brotherhood presence in parliament at that moment as expedient, an implicit warning to the Americans that should they push democracy too far they should be careful, or fearful, of best intentions going awry? In the background, of course, was the victory of the radical Islamic movement Hamas in the Palestinian Authority in the wake of American pressure for free and fair elections. By granting the Muslim Brotherhood one-fifth of the seats, Mubarak was sending his briefly irritated partners in Washington a message via the back door: If you do not want me, you are welcome to the resurgent Islamists, but their agenda (unlike mine) is militantly anti-Israeli and anti-American. The Americans could not have their cake and eat it, too, the regime in effect was saying. It, on the other hand, could square the circle: The Muslim Brotherhood's success at the polls reduced American pressure while Mubarak's regime maintained the crushing pressure on the group's base in the same way that all dissenting protest movements are trampled on by the thuggish state security apparatus, who understand only the politics of violence and repression. Unsurprisingly, in subsequent elections, held after the United States backtracked on its "spreading democracy" campaign, the Muslim Brotherhood failed to win a single seat, despite fielding nineteen candidates.

The starting point for any discussion of the Muslim Brotherhood's influence inside Egypt should therefore be recognition that the number of seats they gain is not necessarily a true reflection of their support; more important is that the vast majority of Egyptians voted neither for them nor for Mubarak's National Democratic Party. Instead, they cast a plague on both parties' houses by stubbornly remaining in their own.

This is not to say that if Mubarak is playing the Brotherhood off against Washington that it is not a dangerous game, nor that Washington has not found its own back against the wall by aiding for a quarter century such an unpopular and uncharismatic dictator who allows only a controlled Islamist opposition symbolically to challenge his authority. In the long term, the Muslim Brotherhood could be a vanguard waiting for the right moment to pounce. As the only organized and disciplined opposition, they would be in the best position to move quickly to fill any vacuum at the center of the Egyptian state should a popular uprising topple the regime, even as it seems clear they would not be the instigators of a revolution.

Media-savvy at home and acute observers of how they are portrayed in the West, their confidence must have been boosted when the Washington-based policy analysts jumped on the bandwagon of Egypt's "Islamist revival," coming as it did on the back of best-selling books like Geneive Abdo's *No God but God: Egypt and the Triumph of Islam* and Mary Anne

Weaver's *A Portrait of Egypt: A Journey Through the World of Militant Islam* (the latter reissued after the September 11, 2001, attacks with "a new chapter on Osama bin Laden") that also presented Egypt as a battleground between Islamists and the dictatorship. This clatter in Washington may have become, albeit inadvertently, part and parcel of Mubarak's political strategy. It helps to drive a self-fulfilling prophecy, whereby the limited support the Muslim Brotherhood has at home is manipulated by the regime to create a false threat, which is then elevated to yet higher significance by commentators abroad.

⌣

The real paradox, though, is the Muslim Brotherhood's own part in this process, and that, I suspect, is the true reason spokesman Hassan did not see the contradiction: To employ its own terminology, the group is very much part of the problem, rather than the solution, when it comes to Egypt's present dire predicament.

Mubarak's exploitation of fears in Washington about the Brotherhood's grassroots presence among some sections of Egypt's poor elevates its status considerably. Add the facts that the group does not have majority support among Egyptians and that the regime nevertheless usefully crushes secularist alternatives while actively encouraging the cultural fascism the Muslim Brotherhood represents, and it becomes obvious why the latter have a vested interest in Mubarak remaining in power, at least until the time is ripe for them to seize it from him during a mass uprising. And what enthusiasm they have shown on occasion to help him achieve that end! Omar Al-Tilimsani, the reformist spiritual guide influential in the 1970s and early 1980s, always stressed the need for the group's official recognition and acceptance, even praising Mubarak as a leader who was bringing more freedom—"a very good, intelligent, clean man who knows what he wants," in his words. In 1987, moreover, the Muslim Brotherhood was the only opposition group in parliament to vote in favor of a second presidential term for their supposed archenemy Mubarak.

This irony—of railing against the rulers while also providing them a service—goes back a long way. It has long been suggested, for instance, that in its early days the Muslim Brotherhood was encouraged by King Farouk and even by the British as a way of countering the influence of the nationalist Wafd Party. Odder still, official documents recently unearthed by scholars researching the Nasser period show that in 1966 this Islamist organization supposedly dedicated to ridding Egypt of foreign influence actually entered into negotiations with the CIA about the chances of a successful Brotherhood-led, anti-Nasser coup.

The Muslim Brotherhood, then, remains a crucial pillar of the establishment rather than its nemesis, ensuring the latter's longevity even as they rail against its incompetence—all in the firm belief that, since God is on their side, they will one day emerge triumphant, and in the meantime can continue to work toward what has always been their most important goal, namely Islamizing Egypt from below. The last piece in this puzzle is the Egyptian people. Hate Mubarak though they may, he knows that for the most part they hate still more the prospect of an Islamist regime that would violate their private (in addition to their public) spheres of existence—thus giving him yet another excuse to play up their significance.

The divergence in Islamist trends in Egypt since the 1970s, between those who advocate violent revolution and those who have rejected violence in favor of gradual reform, is often explained in reference to Sayyid Qutb. Whereas the radical Islamists intent on overthrowing the military regime took Qutb's book *Signposts* (1964) as their manifesto, this argument goes, in rejecting violence the Muslim Brotherhood turned their back on Qutb and instead harked back to the great tradition of liberal Islamic thought that came into its own in Cairo in the late nineteenth and early twentieth centuries, as articulated most famously by Jamal Addin Al-Afghani, Mohammed Abdu, and Rashid Rida. However, as the successful prosecution of Zayid and forced divorce from his wife and the more recent shrill outcry at the mere possibility of a woman not wearing the veil clearly show, the Muslim Brotherhood are far too literal-minded and shallow in their interpretation of Islam and social conventions to be credited with being part of a tradition that emphasized the need, among other things, for an objective and scholarly interpretation of the Qur'an and respect for others' opinions. That third tradition, though, does still exist in Egypt, and has been kept alive mostly by an unlikely individual: Gamal Al-Banna. He is the youngest brother of the assassinated founder of the Muslim Brotherhood, Hassan Al-Banna.

At eighty-five years of age, Gamal Al-Banna has spent much of his life in the study of Islamic texts and emerged against all the odds as a liberal thinker, a man who would like to see Islamic values and practices interpreted in the context of modern times. He was able to devote himself to study because his sister left him plenty of money, thus protecting him from being swept along in the currents of day-to-day politics. Fully conscious of his rare good fortune, he has described himself as "a completely independent man" (he has no family or dependents): "I am not an employee, I am not in any party, and I am not affiliated with anything." Indeed, he did not even go to college after being kicked out of high school due to a dispute with a teacher, and completed his education at a technical school. Instead, he has said, he wanted to write, and write he did. His first book, in 1946, was entitled *A New Democracy,* and one of its chapters was headed "Toward a New Understanding of Islam"—an understanding that came from a man who says he stopped praying for a time in adolescence because he "had no sense of beauty" in the activity and frankly admits that many of the Prophet's quasi-canonical sayings in the sunna were "made up." Yet in a characteristic turn of mind, he said that this does not mean they should be dismissed out of hand, since they laid down important principles. "What it does mean is that it's high time to study the sunna in a different way." In a theocracy, every one of these remarks would get him executed; but this is of no concern to Gamal Al-Banna: "I represent the civil," he says, without vanity, just stating a fact.

I met Gamal in the book-filled office of the Fawziyya and Gamal Al-Banna Foundation that he runs in the Islamic heartland of Cairo. He is indeed *sui generis:* He has a noble head with a great prow of a forehead, aquiline nose, and assertive chin, trailed as might be an ocean liner by the crinkly, regular waves of his receding, swept-back hair—it is uniquely Egyptian hair on an almost pharaonic head. His intellectual independence is of the mild, chuckling, and entirely self-assured variety that must drive opponents to helpless tears of fury. The sense of being in the presence of an exotic saint is strengthened by the dark, carefully tailored, high-collared suits he almost invariably sports as if in outward expression of his lifelong devotion to a religious order of one, religious but modern—it's a suit rather than a robe—and yet not quite like any modern man you've ever met.

The Muslim Brotherhood was founded as a civic institution, with more of a social than a theocratic concept of how Islam should be lived, spread, and interpreted, he told me.

> The difference between me and my brother is the difference between the first and the last, in that Hassan was the first of the brothers in my family

to be born and I was the youngest. There was a fourteen-year gap between us. By destiny, Hassan was from his first days to his last an Islamic
leader, and he was to die as a man of calling. With me, it's a different
story. He was born in the village of Al-Mahmudiya and spent a very idyl-
lic childhood there. He entered the elementary religious school in the village when he was four or five years old, and was recognized as an
unusually intelligent pupil. He was appointed as a teacher in 1927 in the
city of Ismailia, which was where the headquarters of the Suez Canal
Company was located. He studied this city. Soon he discovered that it was
made up of two worlds: one for the top employees of the company, which
was completely European, and the other for the laborers, who were all
Arabs and poor and ignorant.

Hassan Al-Banna had the idea of changing this reality. He went and sat
in the coffee houses, not in the mosque, and from the people he met there
he selected six laborers from the company to form the Muslim Brotherhood in 1928. If Hassan Al-Banna had entered Al-Azhar, then he would
have been completely changed by the environment, his brother suggested,
and would not have been able to launch his movement.

"From the start the Muslim Brotherhood was a community-based
movement," he continued.

This was during the epoch of liberal Egypt, the most brilliant period of
Egyptian history. But when the Muslim Brotherhood was founded, it had
a very simple ideology, and one of the talents of Hassan Al-Banna was
that he could make a very complicated idea very simple and understandable to the masses. He had an extraordinary ability to be able to simplify
difficult and specialist subjects. After some years, the Muslim Brotherhood branched out between Ismailia and Port Said. Then in 1932, Hassan
Al-Banna was transferred to Cairo. In 1948 the Muslim Brotherhood was

launched in Cairo as an international association, to promote Islam as a way of living. That would be the last year of Hassan Al-Banna's life, because he was assassinated in February 1949. But the rapid growth of the Muslim Brotherhood between 1928 and 1948 was proof of his organizational abilities. By the time he died, there were five hundred branches throughout Egypt, and half a million members.

The real story of the rise in their support base was their charity work, he explained.

From the start, in every branch of the Muslim Brotherhood a charitable society was established; and each branch of the charitable society was registered in the Ministry of Social Affairs. Before Hassan Al-Banna, there had been hundreds of Islamic societies, each existing separately from the others; but he established the standard from which all other Islamist movements would later be born—even if they sometimes afterward became independent. In one of my books, I make a comparison between Lenin and Hassan Al-Banna, in the sense that he set up the Bolshevik Party and created an iron-tight bond between the movement and its members.

Coming back to his own relationship with his brother, he said, "It was very dialectic." In every way, Hassan was an Islamic scholar. But the family moved to Cairo when Gamal was four years old and, unlike his brother, he did not enter the village religious school or a school for memorizing and reciting the Qur'an.

Instead, I went to an elementary school that had a secular curriculum. Whereas he was healthy and had a happy, simple childhood by the Nile and under the sun, I was very ill and feeble and had no hobbies other than reading. I was a product of a huge city and not the village, and I read many, many books, and all of them had secular themes. I read about socialism, about constitutional movements in Europe, even about feminism. I stopped praying for a brief period, as many people do when they are young, and I remember Hassan telling me: You have to pray! I told him that I had no sense of beauty in this activity. He replied that I should pray even if the prayer was only performed as a duty. That was an important difference between me and him, although even when we quarreled there was deep fondness in our relationship, real love for one another. Anyhow, my reading gave me a different attitude.

So he represents the civil, while his brother represents the religious.
"I had reservations about the Muslim Brotherhood from the beginning—reservations about their attitude to the role of women, the arts, and politics," he explained.

When I told Hassan Al-Banna about this, he listened and smiled, but he never answered. He was a leader, and it would have been risky to accept these ideas, because the masses wanted simple statements and a leader with a clear vision. The Muslim Brotherhood still has his agenda consisting of all the things I object to: applying strict sharia law, forbidding interest payments by banks, opposition to the arts, and so on. But they have a reformist, not a revolutionary, nature; they do not want power for power's sake, but only as a means of applying sharia. If any other ruler applies sharia, they will applaud him and back him. When Hassan Al-Banna asked me about the slogan "Islam Is the Solution," I told him it is a good slogan, but that is all it is. I understand sharia in a completely different way, a more subtle way. Basically, I understand sharia as meaning justice. If something is not just and has entered sharia it must be put aside, and if something is just but has not entered sharia we must embrace it. I understand this from my reading of the great Islamic scholars of the past. All the other Islamists think only about applying the banalities, such as cutting the thieves' hands and stoning adulterers.

The Muslim Brotherhood and Islamists make use of elections, a Western secular innovation, to win seats in parliament, and then set about imposing their extremist religious agenda on everybody, he insisted.

Still, the Muslim Brotherhood will never be able to apply their preferred strict version of sharia in Egypt if they come to power, because they would be restricted by the Egyptian people, who mostly do not want this. More generally, when they have the challenge of dealing with a complicated reality, they will not be able to solve any of the problems they think Islam is the solution for. They can only thrive in opposition. So the irony is that if they get actual power, it will be the end of them. Who ever liked a government that was ruling them? To survive in power, they would have to make great compromises, even with their deepest held principles. And history is not on their side: All experiments to establish an Islamic state in the modern era have failed, because an Islamic state is not a natural phenomenon. Authority always corrupts religion. Even the early caliphs were corrupted by authority. Without authority, the only virtues the Muslim Brotherhood have are their honesty and their kindness, which no one can deny.

Charity work is still as important to members of the Muslim Brotherhood as preaching, helping the group to appeal beyond its core constituency through a system of wide-ranging social programs. Areas subsidized by the group include education, health, and job training. Countrywide, the

Muslim Brotherhood runs twenty-two hospitals. It also has schools in every governorate. And it runs numerous care centers for poor widows and orphans. Even though the Muslim Brotherhood lacks an official party license, technically banning them from political activity, the social component of their work has largely offset this disadvantage. According to various reports, of the roughly five thousand legally registered NGOs and associations in Egypt, an estimated 20 percent are Brotherhood-run.

In mid-2006 when I visited the Omraniyya Hospital run by the group in a poor area of Cairo a few kilometers from the pyramids, only one room was unoccupied.

"We have close links with the Muslim Brotherhood, and I'm a member of the group," Abdul Hamid Mandy Ismail, the hospital's general manager, said to me as he showed me around.

All twenty-two hospitals are run by the Islamic Medical Committee, which was founded by a former Deputy Supreme Guide and is funded by Islamic charity, Ismail explained.

"We are cheaper than private hospitals, but more expensive than government-run hospitals. However, if someone genuinely cannot pay, we don't charge them anything," he said.

Both Christians and Muslims use the hospital, and women are given treatment whether or not they wear the veil. The exact figures for the percentage of Muslim and Christian patients treated by the hospital are not available, Ismail said, because no one is ever asked about their religious beliefs.

For all the undoubted good they do, the hospitals are nonetheless another example of the Brotherhood's entanglement with the regime. There is a clear contradiction here between banning the group's political arm but allowing it to thrive as a charitable organization. And again, there is a reward in this for both: The Muslim Brotherhood extends its influence, while the government benefits by having others clean up the mess its corrupt mismanagement of the health system created in the first place.

If Washington does decide to listen to the voices of policy analysts inside the Beltway and turn on Mubarak or his successor only in order to cultivate the Muslim Brotherhood, it will not so much mark a "triumph of Islam" but the final death knell for Egypt's deep-set democratic and pluralistic traditions, with devastating consequences for the wider region. Fortunately, saner voices are also there waiting to be heard. In *Whatever Happened to the Egyptians?* sociologist Galal Amin posits, for example, that there are two main reasons Egypt seems to have become more overtly religious in recent decades; they go a long way to explaining the concurrent trends of Islamization from both above and below. "When the economy started to slacken in the early 1980s," he writes, "accompanied by the fall of oil prices and the resulting decline of work opportunities in the Gulf, many of the aspirations built up in the 1970s were suddenly seen to be unrealistic, and intense feelings of frustration followed." A natural tendency toward the stricter observance of religious teaching in the growing sections of society with very modest backgrounds, he adds, "can easily turn to religious fanaticism if associated with severe frustration of earlier hopes of social advancement." He points out, though, that success as well as failure can have the same results, since religious fanaticism can also provide a useful cover for those who have accumulated wealth or income "that is either illegal or immoral"—the greater the degree of corruption, he concludes, the greater degree of religious hypocrisy.

If Amin is right, and a combination of economic mismanagement and blatant corruption are at the root of Egypt's Islamist revival, then the way to combat it is to address the issues that are its cause. It is primarily a case, in other words, of distinguishing the symptoms from the disease. One should perhaps find hope in the fact, too, that the great bulk of the Egyptian population has rejected the Islamist agenda, or at the very least not yet embraced it. If there indeed are grounds for such hope, they may lie in such remnants of the bulging, vital hodgepodge Egypt was in the era of the monarchy that neither the Muslim Brotherhood nor the regime, despite their combined best efforts, has quite managed at the grassroots level to expunge.

CHAPTER THREE

SUFIS AND CHRISTIANS

E gypt is marked by a paradox: The leading political and ideological trends emphasize coherence and unity, and most outsiders tend to think of Egypt as a largely homogeneous country (Muslim, Arab), whereas the reality is that there is considerable diversity that, if allowed to flourish, might create new ideas both politically and economically. For whatever reasons, and there are many, both the ruling regime and its main opposition, the Muslim Brotherhood, emphasize conformity. For the Muslim Brotherhood, this is due, ostensibly, to the concept of *tawhid,* or the unity of Allah, which is extended to a general conception of how society should be organized. In parallel, whether under Nasser or his successors, Al-Sadat and Mubarak, differences are seen not as a source of strength but as a form of weakness. The longstanding justification was the conflict with Israel; a divided enemy is a weak enemy. Even though Egypt is officially at peace with Israel, it is a cold peace and the latter remains a useful cudgel to intimidate and silence views divergent from those officially allowed.

The effects of this attraction to dogma and resistance to diversity will be explored in greater detail in this chapter and the one that follows, but let us first put it into personal perspective. Saad Eddin Ibrahim is an elderly and courtly gentleman, generous of spirit and good humored. He is also an insightful sociologist and arguably Egypt's best-known human rights activist, with connections among numerous journalists and officials. He is also a thorn in the side of the Egyptian government. Throughout the 1990s he was harassed for highlighting discrimination faced by Egypt's ethnic and religious minorities; one conference he organized on the subject was banned at the last minute because it would "tarnish Egypt's image abroad." This, it has to be said, was a rather bizarre but revealing indictment: Apparently pointing out that Egyptians are a diverse people is damaging to Egypt's, or at least the government's, image among others, when one might have thought that diversity is to be respected and a source of pride. Apparently not, given the regime's myth of unity. And apparently not tarnishing to the image of Egypt abroad was the imprisonment and torture of Ibrahim in 2002, when he brought attention to election irregularities and fraud. That on both occasions Egypt was criticized widely for seeking to silence a prominent and well-known critic makes one wonder how concerned the regime truly is about its image. What is certainly clear is that the regime is not terribly concerned about the truth—or perhaps it is really concerned that the truth would be embarrassing to it and tarnish its image abroad. For what lay behind the regime's harassment, at the least, of Ibrahim was his resolve to investigate the vast gap between the regime's claims and reality. And that gap is huge, both when it comes to the regime's claims that Egypt is one and when it comes to its claim that it allows a variety of voices to compete via elections. Indeed, the claim of unity is fundamentally inconsistent with the tenets of democracy, which are based on not only the existence of diversity and differences but also, perhaps of greater importance, their having legitimacy and value.

What is particularly unfortunate about the confluence of the regime's and the Muslim Brotherhood's emphasis on conformity is that the diversity of Egypt is a source of its strength. The benefits of the diverse and cosmopolitan period that preceded the revolution of 1952 were discussed earlier, and one of the sources of nostalgia for that period surely is the dullness of the present Egyptian cultural scene. Yet Egypt remains a vibrant mishmash of different ethnic, religious, and regional groups strongly resistant both to central authoritarianism and bland religious conformity. Such groups include Coptic Christians, who make up between 10 and 15 percent of the population; Upper Egyptians, who maintain tribal kin networks and (in the villages) a system of self-government where not even a local police officer is stationed (a village head instead solves disputes between locals); Sufis who promote personal spiritual enlightenment and communion with God; hundreds of thousands of impoverished Bedouin in the Sinai region, whose own tribal allegiances stretch beyond the border into Israel and who therefore present an ongoing security nightmare for the Egyptian regime; and non-Arab Nubians, who, despite facing an odd combination of sentimental indulgence and crude racism from Arab Egyptians, continue to speak their various maligned languages and keep alive what is left of their unique culture (most of which was lost forever to the depths of the vast lake created with the opening of the High Dam).

How central or marginalized these groups are at any given time is directly related to how authoritarian the Egyptian regime is, and the military establishment that now rules resents those—Egyptians and outsiders alike—who draw attention to their grievances. But these groups together form the majority of Egypt's population. Along with what is left of the liberal intelligentsia and an emerging mass movement of secular labor activism, they offer the only hope that an Egypt may emerge in the future that has as its foundations a celebration of diversity, dignity, and individual human rights. The resistance of Egypt's ethnic and religious groups to the Muslim Brotherhood especially, and the creeping influence of an even more hard-line Wahhabi doctrine imported by Egyptians who emigrated to Saudi Arabia, will have important implications for the wider Arab world, largely under the control of Islamist governments or threatened by popular Islamist movements, and bedeviled by growing Sunni and Shia divisions. One in four Arabs is Egyptian, which is one reason the country has historically been the regional trendsetter. Whether Egyptians choose to embrace dictatorship and iconoclasm, Islamism and uniformity, or democracy and diversity will determine more than just their own fate. And nowhere are the consequences of these choices better illustrated than in the situation faced by Egyptian Sufis and Christians in particular.

Throughout Egypt, multifaceted festivals known as *moulids* are held in honor of holy men and women, both Muslim and Christian (and, until recently, Jewish, too). The objects of veneration include the Prophet and his descendants, the founders of Sufi orders, and dozens of lesser-known sheikhs celebrated mostly in remote rural communities. The biggest moulids, like the one in Cairo held in celebration of Hussein (the second son of the fourth Caliph Ali, whose murder is lamented by the Shia during Ashura), draw crowds of more than a million people. According to the Egyptian Ministry of *Awqaf* (Islamic charity), there are officially more than forty such annual commemorations, with Christians also celebrating their own holy men in huge festivals that similarly can attract hundreds of thousands from across Egypt and the wider Arab world. The Sufi Council in Egypt lists eighty other festivals for lesser-known founders of Sufi orders. The upshot is that at least six million men in Egypt—about a third of the adult male Muslim population—are members of one Sufi order or other; and at least twice that number of men— and countless millions of women and children—participate in the actual festivals the Sufi orders organize. That these figures are likely to surprise outsiders is proof of how the coverage of Egypt in the Western media has tended to favor analyzing developments almost exclusively in relation to the Muslim Brotherhood, to the detriment of other more moderate and mainstream Islamic trends. The Muslim Brotherhood condemns moulids as un-Islamic, and that is one of a number of reasons why they can count such a small number of members in their rank and file—at most about half a million. Praying to holy men and women, even celebrating Muhammad's birthday, is akin to idolatry, according to these Sunni fundamentalists. The sheikhs of Al-Azhar agree with them. However, as the *Christian Science Monitor* noted in October 2006, try as they might, the combined efforts of the Muslim Brotherhood and Al-Azhar to discourage expressions of popular Egyptian Islam "have gained very little traction" among the masses. A senior Brotherhood official "rolled his eyes" when asked about the moulids by the *Monitor*. "We're against it, it's a relic of *jahaliyya*," he told the newspaper, using the Arabic term for the age of "ignorance" before the birth of Islam. "We would really like this to stop," he added. But stopping the phenomenon will be an uphill task. Sufi orders represent the kind of Islam practiced by the majority of Muslims in Egypt. As such, they are the buffer that keeps at bay literalist and extremist interpretations of the faith promoted by the likes of the Muslim Brotherhood. Only rarely during elections does the latter organization even bother with the formality of fielding candidates south of Cairo, where most Egyptians live and where the moulid tradition is most deeply entrenched.

The biggest Egyptian moulid takes place in Tanta, the largest city in the Nile Delta and the country's fifth biggest metropolis. Up to three million Egyptians and other Arabs converge every October in the city to celebrate the life of Sayid Ahmed Al-Badawi, a thirteenth-century Sufi leader. These numbers are staggering: They make the Tanta moulid an even bigger event in the Islamic calendar than the Mecca hajj itself, one of the five pillars of Islam that these days attracts about two million pilgrims from all over the Islamic world. The ostensible aim of those participating in the Tanta moulid, as in all others, is to obtain a blessing from the holy man whose designated day is being marked. The physical centerpiece of any moulid is the holy man's shrine, which is decorated with lights, filled with incense, and open all night to pilgrims. They chant verses from the Qur'an and offer sweets or dabs of perfume to one another. The area surrounding the shrine is transformed into a festival space that can involve the inhabitants of a whole village (or even small city). Groups congregate in tents, which provide space outside for zikr sessions. At a zikr, which means "remembrance" or "commemoration," God is invoked and holy men and women are praised through chanting, singing, and rhythmical swaying.

Tanta's eight-day moulid, which was the first to be established in Egypt, is led by a Sufi leader wearing a turban woven from cloth that once belonged to Al-Badawi himself. The founder of what remains one of Egypt's largest Sufi orders, the Badawiya, was born in Morocco and emigrated to Arabia before moving to Tanta in 1234 to start a new Sufi order. It was a wild celebration from the outset, and has remained a central aspect of life in the area, and the country, ever since. When his tomb was destroyed in the mid-nineteenth century, locals quickly rallied round to build a replacement. The fact that the moulid in Tanta takes place at the end of the cotton harvest illustrates how closely this and many other moulids like it are associated with ancient agricultural rituals. While moulids may mark a saint's birthday, they are just as likely to be held on a day allocated for other, nonreligious reasons. In Upper Egypt, moulids can even mimic ancient pharaonic rites and calendars. They have thus evolved into a kind of all-embracing carnival, and many Egyptians casually accept that their participation in them has less to do with their religious belief than having fun. That is why many Christians hang out with their Muslim friends at Sufi moulids, and many Muslims hang out with their Christian friends at the latter's festivals. Islam has traditionally been practiced in this way by Egyptians, characterized by a tolerance for others, an intense personal spirituality, a strong emphasis on commerce (the moulid is a great opportunity to make money), and—perhaps above all else—a sense of enjoyment.

My own favorite moulid is the one that takes place two weeks before Ramadan to mark the birthday of Abu Al-Hagag, Luxor's patron sheikh—an extraordinary festival that includes horse and camel races, traditional dances, and mock stick fights, all to the accompaniment of music, flashing neon lights, and the endless beating of drums. The festival's highlight is a procession of large boats and other floats through the streets, which resembles the solar processions of the pharaonic era of which Luxor was the very heart. Yussef Abu Al-Hagag (Father of the Pilgrimage), the holy man himself, was born in Damascus in the twelfth century and lived in Mecca before settling in Luxor, where he founded a spiritual retreat. His descendants still live in the area, where (as in the rest of Upper Egypt) the tradition of venerating local sheikhs is especially ingrained into the rural cyclical lifestyle based on the changing of the seasons and thus harvest times. The descendants of Abu Al-Hagag are given pride of place at the front of the street procession, and are easily distinguishable by the flowing white robes and head scarves they alone wear. During Ramadan itself, local

Sufis perform the *zikr* in the evenings outside Abu Al-Hagag's mosque next to Luxor Temple, one of the main pharaonic tourist attractions in the city. Legends abound about the venerable character of this Sufi saint and the lingering power of his spirit. "Last year, just before the moulid, a general from the army came to the mosque and said there would be no moulid unless everything was cleaned up," Hussein, a middle-aged owner of a shop in the local tourist bazaar, told me one year as we watched the parade and threw handfuls of candy at the passing floats crammed with ecstatic and half-naked youths, their torsos covered in bright splashes of paint. "But as the general was pointing to one of the areas around the mosque, he suddenly lost all the power in his arm, and it fell limp by his side," Hussein continued. "At that moment, he admitted defeat. There was a great cheer from the crowd, and as you can see the moulid is going ahead as normal."

How did such moulids become so central a part of life in what officially is a proud Sunni Arab country? Although Egypt's population is indeed now overwhelmingly Sunni, the country's history was interrupted by a Shia period beginning in the tenth century, when the Ismaili Shia, founders of the Fatimid dynasty, conquered and then ruled over Cairo. Al-Azhar mosque, the most important seat of Sunni learning in the Muslim world today, was originally built by the Fatimids to help propagate the Shia faith. That era is very much in the past, of course; but it left a deep imprint on Cairo's architecture and on how Islam is practiced and interpreted in Egypt. The special devotion Egyptians express toward the family of the Prophet (*Ahl Al-Bayt*), and more generally the main Shia saints, is more intense than in any other country in the Sunni Arab world. It is not unusual, for instance, to be introduced to three sons in a single family called Ali, Hussein, and Hassan—names only given to Shia children in a fundamentalist Sunni country like Saudi Arabia. Other Egyptian traditions, such as the sweets eaten during the two Eid festivals to mark the end of Ramadan and the hajj, and the carrying of ceremonial flags denoting Sufi orders during processions during the moulids themselves, are likewise integral aspects of Shia tradition. This history goes a long way to explaining, incidentally, the universal backing inside Egypt for the Shia leader of Hezbollah, Sheikh Hassan Nasrallah, during Israel's bombardment of Lebanon in 2006, despite the Egyptian regime's initial condemnation of Hezbollah's "recklessness" in an attempt to play the sectarian card (and so do America's bidding by trying to turn the Egyptian people against Hezbollah). Notwithstanding the accompanying anti-Shia campaign orchestrated by the goons in the state-run Egyptian media, the overwhelming majority of Egyptians were having none of it. Indeed, a free poster of Nasrallah was distributed by the opposition *Al-Dustour* newspaper during the war, and soon you could find it displayed almost everywhere under the banner headline: "A Symbol of Arab Resistance." Subsequent opinion polls showed Nasrallah to be the most popular Middle East leader among Egyptians. Thereafter, realizing that it had committed a huge political blunder even by its own standards, the regime quickly changed tack, and began instead to condemn Israel's "aggression." The opinion polls revealed, too, that the second most popular leader among Egyptians was Mahmood Ahmadinejad, the president of Shia-majority Iran. That suggests any attempt by the Egyptian regime to mask its backing for a U.S.-led military campaign against Iran in the future by resorting to the sectarian Shia-Sunni divide will also likely backfire, widening still further the yawning gap that already exists between the Mubarak regime and the Egyptian people.

If moulids and their Sufi-Shia origins challenge orthodox Sunni Islam, it naturally follows that the rise of political Islam in Egypt since the 1970s, especially the creeping into the mainstream of the Muslim Brotherhood and its appeasement by the increasingly hard-line Al-Azhar, which is an arm of the regime, could one day threaten the survival of the moulids themselves. This is especially so if the unthinkable happens and the Muslim Brotherhood actually attains power. As fundamentalist thinking has come to dominate the mass media, inevitably it has filtered down to reach some of the Egyptian masses. The result is that increasing numbers are asking whether moulids are in fact *haram* (forbidden) and *bida* (innovation)—two severe violations in strict Islamic law. More generally, the moulid tradition faces other social and spatial marginalization, to the extent that fans of such festivals are becoming nostalgic for moulids past. Many moulid-goers place blame on the state, in addition to the spread of Wahhabi-inspired fundamentalism, for altering the face of these traditional nights of revelry. Anna Madoeuf shows in her essay on moulids in the excellent book *Cairo Cosmopolitan* (2006), edited by Diane Singerman, that state policies have certainly played a part. Increasingly heavy-handed attempts by Cairo city police and the national government to close down public spaces to hugely popular Sufi festivals, she notes, "is as a way to repress large-scale public gathering," particularly "after large public protests in Cairo after the 2003 U.S. invasion of Iraq." However, the reasons behind the growing hostility to moulids are more subtle and complex than just the government's dislike of street merchants or anxiety about large crowds. That, for example, hardly explains acts of sabotage by Sunni extremists at some moulids.

At one moulid in Upper Egypt a few years ago, while religious songs were being performed on stage at night a rumor spread through the crowd that a local boy had been kidnapped. "The moulid was just about ruined," an attendee from a nearby village told the now-defunct magazine *Cairo Times,* which had unearthed the story as part of a feature on the threats moulids face in Egypt today. "Things were a bit chaotic. A lot of people went home to see what was going on and the singer rushed and finished early. It was a small moulid to begin with, so news like that was enough to spoil everything," he added. But the kidnapped boy, it later turned out, was an active member of an Islamist group, and one of many conservative locals who opposed the moulid's having taken place. He reappeared two days later, recovering from his "ordeal" in bed, although his health apparently seemed fine. According to the *Cairo Times* article, many villagers later claimed that the kidnapping had been acted out to put a dampener on the moulid festivities. "It was all a fantasy, a farce they weren't even able to plot well. He was 'kidnapped' on the night of the moulid itself, and there was no talk at all as to what the kidnappers wanted, why they kidnapped him, or what interest it served," another villager claimed. The activists were reportedly upset that the local tradition was being revived after a lack of organization had resulted in a moulid-free period for several years. They had tried to convince residents that celebrating moulids was a sin. Frustrated at their failure to dissuade the villagers from participating, they apparently resorted to the fake kidnapping to undermine the celebration. Moulid sabotage undertaken in a similar spirit is still remembered by the Nile Delta villagers of Jizaya. In the mid-1990s, during moulid Al-Nabi, which marks the Prophet's birthday, the village square's ornamental banners, lights, poles, and speakers were found to have been taken down two mornings in a row, and a flag embroidered with religious phrases went missing. Undeterred, the Sufi organizers reassembled the festive props and continued their celebrations. But on the third morning, they found that a pole and banner removed from the festive space had been thrown into an open sewer.

What seems especially to irritate fundamentalists is the casual mixing of men and women during moulids, and this points to the growing influence of Saudi Arabia's state ideology, Wahhabism, on Egyptian cultural life since the 1970s, when millions of Egyptians started to migrate to Saudi

Arabia to work as a result of the oil boom. Often, they took their wives and children with them, and the children were enrolled local schools that do little other than propagate Wahhabi doctrine. The workers themselves, often poorly educated or illiterate and so susceptible to indoctrination, became immersed in the extremist Wahhabi ideology that pervades Saudi mosques and society, and which damns, among other things, both the mixing of the sexes and the moulid tradition of worshipping saints (both of which, along with just about everything else, are banned in Saudi Arabia). Egypt is historically liberal in terms of its politics, global in terms of its cultural outlook, moderate in its interpretation of religion, and embracing of diversity of opinion. Saudi Arabia, in contrast, has always been conservative politically, completely closed to outside cultural expression, extremist in its interpretation of Islam, and severely discouraging when it comes to the question of dissenting personal opinion.

One can but reflect on how beneficial it would have been for the Arab world if Egyptians had exported their own Sufi Islam as they descended by the millions on Saudi Arabia, rather than in so many instances bringing the Wahhabi ideology back with them to their home country. This is especially so considering that the ongoing cultural and religious conflict between Egypt and the Al-Saud royal family, which the moulids provide just one battleground for, dates back to the reign of Mohammed Ali in the early nineteenth century, when he received orders from the Ottoman Sultan to expel the Al-Saud family and their Wahhabi allies from Mecca, then a semiautonomous region under Ottoman control but which the Al-Saud had managed to occupy. Mohammed Ali carried out the mission with complete success, even chasing the fanatical Wahhabis back to their stronghold in the central Arabian region of Al-Najd, where he slaughtered most who had escaped from the initial battle in the Hijaz. Thus Mohammed Ali provided a great service to Islam by liberating Mecca from the Wahhabi fanatics. Alas, after the collapse of the Ottoman Empire following the First World War the Al-Saud regained control of the holy cities of Mecca and Medina and other provinces of the Saudi kingdom, which was officially unified and named Saudi Arabia in 1932. Until the 1920s, at the beginning of the annual hajj Egyptians had carried the black cloth that covers the Kaaba in the holy mosque in Mecca, to the accompaniment of religious music and Sufi dancing and rejoicing. After the Al-Saud consolidated their rule over the Hijaz in the mid-1920s, however, the Egyptians were pelted with stones and damned as idolaters, and the tradition of carrying the cloth came to an abrupt end. After the discovery of the vast lake of oil underneath Saudi Arabia, Wahhabism, funded by an Al-Saud family suddenly flush with cash, spread like wildfire throughout the Islamic world, including into some sections of the Egyptian society. It found especially fertile ground with the rise of Islamism in the 1970s under Al-Sadat and his encouragement of the Muslim Brotherhood to return from exile in Saudi Arabia. The importance to the Egyptian economy of remittances from Egyptians working in Saudi Arabia further encouraged the Egyptian regime's passivity in the face of the rise of Saudi Arabia.

There is a bigger story here, of course, namely how Egypt has gradually abandoned its historic role as leader of the Arab world since 1967 and instead taken a backseat to Saudi Arabia, both in terms of religion and politics. If in retrospect Nasser's pan-Arabism seems to have given Arabs little to celebrate, it is certain nothing good can come from the Arab world as long as the fanatical Wahhabis of Saudi Arabia are in control. For Egypt, the results of the spread of Wahhabism are already evident. As we have seen, the condemnation by a minority of Wahhabi-inspired zealots of popular moulids as un-Islamic is one. The singling out for discrimination and violence of Egypt's Christian minority, also damned as infidels by Wahhabi doctrine, is another.

Oddly, it was on a trip to the heart of Upper Egypt to visit a friend's village about half-an-hour from the industrial city of Sohag, while a moulid festival was taking place there, that I got a first-hand glimpse into the plight of Egypt's Coptic Christian community. During a walk around the village on the first day, my friend's father, a headmaster at the local school, made a point of emphasizing the friendships that existed between his Muslim friends and the local Copts, often pointing the Copts out after they had exchanged greetings in the street. But when we made a series of visits to the houses of his friends as darkness fell and the moulid preparations got underway, it turned out that none of them were Copts. And later, when I asked my friend whether there had ever been any disturbances between the two communities in the village, he let slip that a few years back there had indeed been considerable tension because the Copts had briefly asserted on their right to build a church (they presently have to make do instead with a converted house).

"Would that really have caused so much trouble?" I asked.

"Yes, it would," he said. "This is a Muslim country."

"What would have happened if they had insisted on building it?" I wanted to know.

The coldness of his reply was chilling: "We would have beaten them."

The limits to the communal "friendship" were clear: Coptic Christians were treated with respect, so long as they accepted their status as second-class citizens. That these limits came from "moderate" Muslims whose own popular festive traditions—the moulid drew almost all of the Muslims in the village out of their homes that evening—were under threat from hard-line Sunni Islam indicated that the Copts were right at the bottom of the local pecking order. I noticed the roots of this discrimination on the road out of the village the following day. As in the village itself, all of the homes we passed in the taxi were modern, red-brick constructions—hardly the mud-brick, poverty-stricken image of Upper Egypt conjured up by those who talk of the government's neglect of the region. Where, I wanted to know, had they managed to get the money? Almost all of the men, my friend told me, worked in the Gulf, and he was hoping to travel to Saudi Arabia too once he had finished his studies.

"We didn't witness any sectarian trouble in Egypt until about thirty years ago," Georgette Kallini, a Coptic member of the governing National Democratic Party twice appointed to the People's Assembly by Mubarak, told me when I met up with her later in Cairo and relayed my experiences in the village. It seemed to strike her as a depressingly familiar tale. "It started when Muslim Egyptians, especially from Upper Egypt, began to travel to Saudi Arabia and other Gulf states to find work during the 1970s oil boom," she explained in English, which she spoke with a heavy French accent. Many, she continued, returned with a new extremist "Wahhabi mindset" alien to Egypt's historically tolerant religious and cultural environment, and which tells Muslims they are superior to non-Muslims. She claimed the impact of such thinking "was especially combustible in Upper Egypt, which already was a very tribal society." There was also the growth during the same decade of a home-grown movement of political Islam preached by the Muslim Brotherhood, which Al-Sadat had courted to help marginalize leftists. "When Egypt's Christians suddenly heard their endlessly repeated slogan, Islam is the Solution, they shuddered, and felt further alienated from the mainstream," she said, suppressing a shudder herself as she spoke. "Our constitution says that all citizens of Egypt are equal, but the reality is different. I could give the example of how, if a Muslim owner of an institution has four positions open, he almost always would employ four Muslims. If we are all equal, shouldn't it go to the best person, regardless of religion?"

These days violence between Muslim and Coptic Egyptians is forever threatening to spiral out of control. "The biggest danger in Egypt right now is that of festering sectarian conflict," Ragaa Attiya, a member of Al-Azhar University's Islamic Research Centre, has been quoted as saying. In the most dramatic incident in 2006, knife-wielding Muslims in Alexandria attacked worshippers at Coptic churches. A seventy-eight-year-old Christian died and several others were injured. During the funeral procession for the dead man, clashes broke out between Muslims and Christians. One Muslim died, more than forty people of both faiths were wounded, and dozens more were arrested. According to a report for Middle East Report Online at the time, the next day street fighting erupted again, this time after Christians marched down one of Alexandria's main thoroughfares bearing crosses and shouting Christian slogans. The Muslim neighborhood in Alexandria where the church attacks took place has long been a hotbed of Saudi-style Islam.

However, many Christians and Egyptian human-rights monitors also point fingers of blame at their own government. Their theory could only have been reinforced when Hala Helmy Boutros, a Coptic from Upper Egypt, started a blog to draw attention to what she described as anti-Coptic harassment and violence. She soon found herself to be a symbol of just that—after her blog was closed down, her movements were tracked by the secret police, and her telephone and e-mail messages bugged. Finally, a group of thugs—thought to have been hired by the local government—told her father while beating him up: "This is a present from your daughter." But there are others who counter that such forms of state violence ultimately have little to do with religion. "I'm a Copt and I live happily in a neighborhood full of Christians and Muslims," said George Ishaq, the founder of the opposition Kifaya pro-democracy movement that calls for the peaceful overthrow of the Mubarak regime. "Police respond in a heavy-handed way to any public disturbance. That's always what makes everything spiral of out control."

Still, other longstanding Coptic complaints include the under-representation of Christians in the police, judiciary, armed forces, civil service, government, and education system. There is also a virtual ban on access to state-controlled radio and television. One oft-cited example of official discrimination is a law that, until recently, required personal presidential approval to carry out even simple church repairs, such as fixing a toilet, and which was blamed for delays of more than a decade in the issuing of permits to build churches. Mubarak eased the law in 2005, delegating such responsibility to local governors. This provoked a mixed reaction from activists, with the influential Coptic Christian weekly *Watani* calling it a sham that merely aimed to appease foreign critics. But Copts, too, should acknowledge a growing isolationist trend within their own flock, other Muslim and Christian intellectuals argue. They find especially offensive a program on the Coptic satellite station Al-Hayat that is hosted by a certain Father Zakaria Boutros, an Egyptian priest repeatedly arrested by the regime when he lived in Egypt but who now lives in exile in the United States. In his popular, hour-long Sunday show, he throws crude insult after crude insult at Islam, the Qur'an, and Prophet Muhammad, all of which have provoked strong condemnation from none other than the head of the Coptic Church in Egypt, Pope Shenouda. Figures like Father Zakaria certainly feed notions of foreign plots against "national unity" that have been abuzz in Egypt's media since a forum on the Coptic question was held in the United States in November 2005. Organized in part by associations of Coptic émigrés, its theme was that "democracy in Egypt should benefit Christians as much as Islamists." The immediate context of the conference, according to a Middle East Report Online article, was the rise of Islamists in politics after the country's parliamentary elections; but it was also a testimony to the rising profile of U.S.-based Coptic groups. According to the article, such groups have found willing support in U.S. neo-conservative and evangelical Christian circles. In fact, publicity for the event was handled by Benador Associates—a public relations firm known for its roster of neo-conservative clients.

Now at the center of various conspiracy theories is the U.S.-educated and most controversial figure in the Coptic community today: Bishop Max Michel. Some years ago, he moved to the United States to pursue postgraduate studies at St. Elias School of Orthodox Theology. He says he earned his doctorate in divinity in 2004. In July 2005 he was ordained a bishop by the Holy Synod for the American Diaspora of True Orthodox Christians, a group of Old Calendarists based in Nebraska. A year later, he was promoted to the rank of archbishop by the same synod, and took the regal name of Maximus I. After returning to Egypt, the fifty-seven-year-old bishop proclaimed himself the Archbishop of Orthodox Christians of Egypt and the Middle East, an explicit challenge to the authority of Pope Shenouda, whose full title is the 117th Pope of Alexandria and Patriarch of the See of St. Mark. He then announced that he was establishing a new Holy Orthodox Synod. An official invitation to attend the July 4th (Independence Day) celebrations at the U.S. Embassy in Cairo followed, according to *Egypt Today,* raising questions about the U.S. position on the issue. However, U.S. Ambassador to Egypt Francis Ricciardone later issued a statement denying that the United States was supporting Michel.

Michel voices blunt criticism of Pope Shenouda and the administrative order of the Coptic Orthodox Church, which he says is similar to "medieval Inquisition churches" in dealing with those who hold opinions different from their own. "The attitude and behavior inside the (Coptic) church is the same as it was in the Middle Ages," he told me at his St. Athanasius Church in Cairo, dressed in papal robes. "The only authority is for the pope. He must be obeyed. We should go back to what the original founding fathers of the Orthodox Church say, not to what this pope says. Even the congregations are told not to buy certain newspapers that are critical of Pope Shenouda, and they are told that if they do buy them they will no longer be accepted into the Church," he added. Egypt's Coptic Orthodox Church said in a statement: "Max Michel was appointed by people who have abandoned the Orthodox Church . . . and therefore the Church does not recognize his authority." The spokesman for the Coptic Orthodox Cathedral in Cairo, Salib Mata Sawiris, told journalists there was the possibility that such a "split" was indeed backed by the United States in its efforts to hurt Pope Shenouda's popularity. But Michel denied any ties to the U.S. government. "The only ties I have are with the friends I made during my days as a student, and some Egyptians I met who live in America," he told me.

According to *Egypt Today,* Michel departs from the teachings of the Orthodox Church on three major points. While the Orthodox Church insists that divorce is permissible only in cases in which one spouse embraces another faith or in the case of grievous adultery, Michel contends that there are at least eight grounds on which the faithful can request a divorce. He also conducts pilgrimages to holy sites in Jerusalem and the occupied West Bank, a ritual banned by Pope Shenouda, who has said that the Church will not normalize relations with Israel until there is a lasting settlement to the Israeli-Palestinian conflict. Michel also contends that there are no religious grounds prohibiting bishops from marrying. He himself is married, with two children, although under Coptic canon law only unmarried priests are eligible for appointment to the rank of bishop.

Michel is confident that the Egyptian government will formally approve recognition of his new church. A year after it was established, he said, it already has a dozen branches all over the country and thousands of followers. But he is sure to continue to face strong opposition, not only from within the Coptic Church and in the civil law courts, but also from mainstream Coptic voices. Coptic business leader heavyweight Mounir Fakhry Abdel-Nour rallied against Michel after he returned to Egypt, calling him a "charlatan."

CHAPTER FOUR

THE BEDOUIN

I n October 2007, thousands of angry Bedouin rampaged through the streets of Al-Arish on the Sinai peninsula, shattering pictures of Mubarak, smashing furniture in the local branch of the National Democratic Party, burning tires in the streets, throwing stones, shooting guns in the air, and breaking shop windows. Police eventually used tear gas to break up the protests. The official media insisted the trouble was the result of a feud between two Bedouin tribes, the Tarabin and Fawakhriya, which arose after a shooting incident in which three people were wounded as they left a mosque after prayers. "An isolated local incident," the governor of Al-Arish called it; and the official press duly reported that the Tarabin were only angry at the state for failing to protect them from the Fawakhriya. But only two weeks earlier, hundreds of Bedouin had blocked the main road leading to Sharm Al-Sheikh with burning tires and stone barricades, and that time they were protesting the demolition of twenty houses the authorities claimed had been built without a permit. A few days later, there were more protests in Al-Arish by the

Bedouin demanding that the authorities release Bedouin prisoners—some of whom they alleged had been detained without trial since 2004 when terrorist attacks in Taba marked the first of a series of bombings of the shiny new Red Sea resorts that now account for a sizable chunk of Egypt's tourist industry. It also marked the return of terrorism to Egypt after seven quiet years.

In Taba there is much glitz and glamour, with spanking new hotels often geared to a new wave of European tourists and moneyed Israelis, part of a planned Egyptian Riviera that would stretch all along the coast to Aqaba. Egypt had been anxious to oblige both groups: The developers had moved in to build huge, integrated complexes with their waterslides and faux-Andalusian design that pushed out the established local businesses. It was all, in its way, much the same depressing story as development in Cairo after the 1952 coup. In October 2004, the terrorists chose their target with care: They bombed one of the most conspicuous of consumption sites, not only an archsymbol of the global tourist industry but also the preferred accommodation for Israeli tourists: the Taba Hilton. The attack claimed thirty-four lives, many of them Israeli. Then, in July 2005, bombs exploded in the biggest and longest established of the Red Sea resorts, Sharm Al-Sheikh, killing some eighty people at the height of the season. But these were mostly Egyptians. And in April 2006, it was the turn of Dahab, where triple bombings killed nineteen Egyptians. Yet Cairo's reaction was the same in each case: mass arrests—reportedly thousands of Bedouin were rounded up, and many tortured—and vague denunciations of Al-Qaeda that would, of course, have been music to the ears of Mubarak's paymasters in Washington.

After a confused investigation, the government eventually fingered a hitherto unknown group called Gamaat Al-Tawhid wa Al-Jihad. A statement obtained by the Egyptians from a leader of the organization seems to make it clear that it was essentially a Palestinian Islamist group and that some of the attackers had been trained in Palestine (all its leaders were killed or surrendered, apparently fatally weakening the group). A well-known independent, nonprofit organization based in the United States called the International Crisis Group (ICG), in an outstanding report on the Sinai question published in January 2007, says there is "good reason" to assume that the first attack did have a Palestinian link, given the many Israeli victims; but the second and third attacks could suggest that the terrorists were in fact "sending a message to Mubarak": The main bombing target in Dahab was perhaps not coincidentally owned by a local who had made major contributions to Mubarak's election campaign.

At best, the situation is a mess. And it still begs the question: Why Cairo's brutal crackdown specifically on the Bedouin of the Sinai?

Covering some 61,000 square kilometers, the Sinai peninsula extends from the Mediterranean coast to the Gulf of Suez and the Gulf of Aqaba, forming a frontier province at the junction of Africa and Asia. It has always been a strategic buffer between the Nile Valley and Egypt's eastern neighbors. As early as the rule of Muhammed Ali in the first part of the nineteenth century, control of Sinai was a vital matter from the moment he began to assert his autonomy from his Ottoman masters by building a centralized state and defining its borders. The opening of the Suez Canal in 1869 put the region at the heart of attempts by European powers to control trade between the Red and Mediterranean Seas. In the first Taba Treaty of

1906, the British, who had imposed their mandate over Egypt since 1882, won the official unification of the peninsula with the Egyptian protectorate and drew the border with Palestine. Henceforth it was administered by the British army, and it has been under varying forms of military control ever since.

In many ways the Suez Canal remains the real eastern border of Egypt, and Sinai is what the ICG report called a "semi-detached" region. Between 1949 and 1967, Sinai and the Gaza Strip came under Egyptian military administration, with the difference that Egypt claimed sovereignty over Sinai only. Then came the Yom Kippur War, and both fell to Israel, becoming a symbol of wounded Arab pride. The Camp David Agreement between Israel and Egypt in September 1978 and the March 1979 peace agreement naturally put Sinai at the heart of negotiations. For Egypt, it was a question of reconquest and national affirmation, quite disconnected even from the Israeli-Palestinian conflict. In short, Sinai had turned into an abstract concept. The long and difficult diplomacy to recover the Taba enclave alone showed how much Egypt cared—about the territory, that is, not necessarily about its people. Eventually, the peninsula was demilitarized and occupied by a U.S.-dominated multinational force, which began its work in 1982, the day Israeli troops withdrew from Sinai. To this day, it remains under the special security regime mandated by the peace treaty, which significantly qualifies Egypt's freedom of military action there.

Yet Sinai is neither an abstract concept nor a "terrorist problem." Historically, it is the land of the *bedu*, the people of the desert. The tribes originally came from the Arabian peninsula and the countries of the Levant. Some fifteen major tribes now share Sinai, in territories demarcated and governed by agreements between groups under customary tribal law rather than the laws of their overlord. One of the tribes, the Al-Azazma, is divided between Jordan, Syria, Palestine, and Egypt. The Al-Azazma claim rights to all the land from Bier Sanaa to the Araba valley west of Egypt, in addition to some land in the Sinai desert, and dominate Central Sinai together with the Tayaha and Ahaiwat tribes. In the northeast, along the Mediterranean, are the Sawarka and the Rumaylat, now mostly settled in Al-Arish, Sheikh Zweid, and Rafah. To the west, the majority are the Masaid, the Bayyadiyya, and the Dawaghra. In the south, the majority groups are the Tuwara, a confederation of tribes including the Alaiqa, Awlad Said, and Muzaina, who live in the Sharm Al-Sheikh region, in the mountains of the interior, and especially in the Dahab area. The Tarabin, the group at the center of the recent disturbances, are another important group historically both in Nuwaiba and, above all, in the north, extending as far as Israel and the West Bank.

But the people generally described as Bedouin are really "a mosaic of populations reflecting the complex settlement history of the peninsula," as the ICG report pointed out—with clear distinctions in terms of origins, traditions, economic activities, and even language: They are from everywhere. The Jibaliyya are not even Arabs, but rather are thought to come from Macedonia, sent to Sinai by the Ottomans to ensure security. There they converted to Islam and are now identified as Bedouin, but they maintain their separate identity through an incongruous attachment to the monastery of St. Catherine (a major tourist attraction located at the foot of Mount Sinai, where Moses is said to have revealed the Ten Commandments) and a claim over the district and the tourist routes. Others can be clearly distinguished by dialects that are close to those of the Levant or the Arabian peninsula, but which also distinguish the tribes from one another. Some came from as far south as Nuba, which historically stretched from Aswan into Sudan. Nobody knows how many of them there are. Estimates run to some two hundred thousand among a total population of approximately three hundred thousand six hundred for the entire Sinai peninsula.

The rest are mostly Palestinians, with their equally strong sense of identity. Yet census data from 1995 show only a few thousand people identified as Bedouin residing in the south, mostly farmers and fishermen but also a few lucky traders and civil servants. This is because an estimated seventy-five thousand Bedouin have no citizenship at all: The government has at most granted some of them Sinai identification papers. Among the tribes ignored by the government, according to various reports, are the Al-Rashida in Halayeb and Shalatin, who originally came from Qatar and moved later to Sudan and Egypt, where they settled around the Nile, southern Egypt, and parts of the Red Sea; the Al-Tafilat in southern Sinai; and the Malaha in Rafah on the Gaza-Egypt border. One tribal leader told the newspaper *Al-Khamiss* that the complications surrounding citizenship went back to the days of the first Taba Treaty of 1906. "The treaty said all those who live in Egypt must hold Egyptian citizenship, and when the English army did the first census in 1924, all the tribes were given identification papers"— except, that is, for those who were not.

While their land is mostly a chessboard in the eyes of their rulers, and they have been an annoyance to Nasser's monoethnic dream of a centralized Egypt, the Bedouin have nonetheless served a variety of useful functions for their various governments. Historically, their knowledge of desert travel made their caravans the lifeline of many economies, a purpose that can still be traced today: When Libya opened its borders to the United Nations, for instance, the World Food Program contracted with a Bedouin tribe to transport supplies for Sudanese refugees from the Mediterranean port of Benghazi down through the trackless desert to the camps of eastern Chad. Of course, they also have a reputation as warriors and have allowed themselves to be recruited as mercenaries for generations. Modern nations still rely on them for territorial security: The first king of Saudi Arabia, King Abdul Aziz, married a woman from the powerful Shammar tribe to secure his northern borders.

But in that usefulness also lay the roots of their problems, for if their loyalty could be bought by one group, the emerging nation-states felt, it could be bought by someone else as well. And they know that tribal loyalties have always taken precedence over abstract notions like national identity: The borders that modern nation-states fight and negotiate over mean little compared to the centuries-old tribal land rights of which the Bedouin say they are systematically being deprived.

Every country in the Middle East with a Bedouin population has tried to settle them, much as European governments have tried to settle the Roma; but the Egyptian government, being what it is, has tried to alter their lifestyle by brute muscle. The newspaper *Al-Wafd* best reflected the government's somewhat deranged enthusiasm when it wrote that a regional agricultural development strategy would provide "not only a gold mine," which some private investors could monopolize, but above all "would permit the construction of a security cordon along Egypt's open frontier"—note that the Bedouin are seen as mere building blocks for the construction of a cordon—in that the policy could "convert immense areas into something resembling colonies in the desert, which would form a barrier against terrorists and conspirators entering Egypt."

Urban expansion on traditional grazing lands and drought caused by erratic weather in recent decades have led to the loss of much of the livestock of those Bedouin who still herded it—in some cases of entire tribal herds—who are the poorest and most marginalized. But the Bedouin are equally "locked out" of the tourism boom. During the last fifteen years, all building plots in the Red Sea resorts were allocated to Arab Egyptian and foreign firms investing in tourism, while the Bedouin were, through government programs, packed off to the desert. Unemployment rates among the Bedouin are extremely high, and most are denied the education and skills to start small businesses catering to tourists. In 2002 alone, one hundred and ten hotels created between ten and thirty thousand direct jobs; but nearly every one went to Egyptians from elsewhere. To ease the unemployment in Cairo and the crowded cities of the Nile Delta, the state is actively encouraging workers to move from there to Sinai, where they enjoy better pay and living conditions; and the Bedouin they push out have to look for alternative ways to make a living, which prove almost nonexistent in the area—at least legal ones. According to the ICG, of the two hundred and fifty employees of one five-star hotel all are from the Nile Valley—with the exception of two sailors on the boat staff, who come from the governorate's administrative capital of Al-Tur. The Bedouin are now even prohibited from working as tour guides on desert roads.

Consider the case of the coastal village of Garghana. The Bedouin there live near mangrove forests that are in principle well worth saving for the good of the local ecosystem. During the summer, they rely on fishing as their primary source of livelihood, and they preserve fish for the winter, when they move to a wadi to escape the cold and strong winds of the coast. Now the Bedouin say they are systematically being isolated and marginalized for the sake of a new ecotourism industry that has sprung up all over South Sinai. First, they claim, the resort and hotel operators wanted to prohibit them from fishing, so the Bedouin agreed to fish only in designated grounds imposed by the South Sinai Protectorate; then the governor was accused of completely banning them from fishing anywhere. They are continuously being pushed into the hinterland. For some younger people, the start of ecotourism and the money it made changed their perspective: They tried to adapt so as not to be left out; but at the expense, their elders feel, of the integrity of their traditional values: simplicity, cohesiveness, respect for traditional tribal organization, and the rhythms of their traditional life. In short, they turned to hustling and to crime. Any sensible development, of course, would have tried to integrate the fishing Bedouin into the tourism projects, for the sake of the cash to be made from picturesque experiences among the natives if nothing else; but in fairness, much of the rest of the world, too, is only beginning to wake up to any options that go beyond exhibiting a handful of giraffe-necked women to gaping tour groups.

In southern Sinai, nonetheless, that is how many Bedouin can still scrape by on the margins of the tourist industry: by turning themselves into an attraction. Regardless of their marginalization, the official tourist brochures are full of pictures of colorful Bedouin. But in northern Sinai, there is hardly any tourism. Tourist villages built by the Egyptian government along the northern coast are effectively ghost towns, and the small Al-Arish industrial zone and the airport are not enough to support the Bedouin families. Promises of new projects and financial aid for housing or employment have, as the Israeli newspaper *Ha'aretz* put it in an October 2007 article, "turned into a joke." As ever in Egypt, there were grand plans and feasibility studies, but in reality no large factories have been built since 2001, and the total number of people employed in the factories that already exist is reported to be less than five thousand. That is not to say that settlement efforts have not worked: They have, but not in the way the government intended. "The social and economic changes in the peninsula during the last fifteen years, combined with the high population growth rate," writes the ICG, "have resulted in *de facto* settlement on the urban periphery by Bedouins seeking jobs and schooling for their children." In other words, they have created a suburban underclass, with all the new problems—of crime and radicalization of the young—that entails.

Nor is the education they go in search of there necessarily worth finding. The rural Bedouin not registered as citizens have no access to public education at all. According to development agencies, illiteracy is as high as 90 percent among some sectors of the Bedouin population. And if they do find access, it is centered as in all Egypt—but quite irrelevantly to the Bedouin—on the pharaonic heritage and the central state. If there has been one project the government has pursued with some zest, it was to establish a pharaonic museum in Al-Arish: Given the area's nonexistent heritage in that regard, it seems nothing more than an attempt to impose the state's stamp on a town that until then had a thriving Bedouin museum. And when parents privately teach their children about their Arab heritage, they are sometimes reportedly called in by the teachers.

On the political front, the regime's mistake has meanwhile been to imagine its own military structure reflected in the tribal setup: Get a handle on the man in charge, its reasoning has been, and you have a handle on the whole. Thus state security has started playing a role in how tribal sheikhs are chosen, which was traditionally done by tribal consensus, just as Cairo now insists that all imams must be government employees. In reality, the new imams have no credibility among the masses, and the new chiefs no credibility among the tribes, and the weakening of their influence in both instances has left a vacuum that could be filled by extremists. The sheikhs' legitimacy has been compromised to the point where they are beginning to play a similar role to those of Saudi Arabia, whose professed loyalty to the regime obscures a quite different reality among the rank and file.

The neglect is a vicious cycle.

"For years now life has been rendered unbearable for us, and it seems that any Bedouin is considered suspect by default," an unnamed tribal member told *Al-Ahram Weekly* in May 2007. The distrust was cemented in the years of the Israeli occupation of Sinai, when the Bedouin were seen as Israel's allies and therefore as traitors to the Egyptian national cause. Perhaps understandably, that label stuck after the return of Sinai to Egypt. Across the border, after all, the Israeli army maintains an entire battalion of local Bedouin, some of them tribal cousins of those in Egypt, and roughly 20 percent of eligible young men volunteer. Historically, Bedouin towns in Israel have therefore voted heavily for Zionist parties, with hard-liners winning up to 95 percent of the Bedouin vote in some towns as recently as the 1980s. That has declined for several elections, but Jewish right-wingers still win the majority of ballots of the Bedouin. The notorious Bedouin Reconnaissance Battalion is largely responsible for patrolling the border areas, and until Israel pulled out of Gaza it had a presence along the Rafah border as well. Palestinians say Israel's Bedouin soldiers are much more aggressive and brutal than the Israeli Defense Forces, for it is they who drive the demolition trucks. The young British peace activist Tom Hurndall, who died defending a Palestinian house from demolition in Rafah in 2004, was shot dead by an Israeli Bedouin soldier who was later convicted.

After the recent riots, there were predictably reports in Cairo's patriotic press that the Bedouin were asking to be annexed back to Israel or to create an "autonomous entity" for themselves. In a manifesto published in Al-Arish, the tribal heads stressed that they considered themselves "loyal citizens of Egypt" and there should be no doubt about their national affinity. And the sheikh of the Al-Azazma told reporters: "We are Egyptian in spite of the government's negative attitude toward us, we are patriots despite of the way we are treated by the state security, and we ask President Mubarak to help us out." Even if that were true, there are few in Cairo willing to listen: much better to blame the violence on the notoriously disloyal, scrappy tribes than admit there is a genuine problem the government might have helped to create. Instead, the press kept harping on an interview another Bedouin representative had given to the BBC Arabic channel, where he explained that the Bedouin had gone to Israel to convey their concerns to the Egyptian ambassador in Tel Aviv, "because it's closer to us than Cairo." He probably meant closer physically—the Bedouin did not after all go marching into the Knesset—but this could still be sold as a traitorous request for Israeli involvement.

Not that one could blame them. Israel may let the Bedouin do its dirty work, but at least it pays them; whereas it must be difficult for even the most loyal sheikh to explain to his tribe why exactly he is fond of the Egyptian state, except perhaps to point out that what binds them to other Egyptians is the torture the state so liberally metes out to them as well. In reality, however, they are not enamored of either side. On the one hand, their wretched standard of living and the pervasive suspicion they face has prompted some Bedouin to find alternative livelihoods in the form of drug dealing, trafficking of women to Israel—a way station for prostitutes from Eastern Europe and Central Asia—and weapons trading with the Palestinians. It is not as if they have a reputation to lose.

The Bedouin along the porous border do regularly cross back and forth, and accusations of smuggling by the governments of both Egypt and Israel are well founded. In September 2007, Egyptian authorities uncovered a munitions cache that contained about three tons of explosives stored in plastic bags, and in July of the same year a ton and a half of explosives were discovered just twenty-five kilometers from the border with Gaza. At the same time, Islamism—and thus hatred of Israel—has apparently found a fertile breeding ground among the younger Bedouin, fueled by the identity politics that will inevitably flare up among people with their backs to the wall. The ICG report quotes one man from Nuwaiba, who is representative of many, as saying: "I am a Muslim, an

Arab, a Tarabin Bedouin, from Sinai and from Egypt." So religion comes first, partly because many of the tribes trace their origins back to the land of the Prophet, as opposed to the land of the pharaohs. How much of that is lip service to the religion—whether, in other words, the tribe does not really still come first—and to what extent being Arab means not being Jewish or Western is impossible to tell; either way the power of Islam is unmistakable. Add poverty and disaffection into the mix, and the result is predictable.

"The itineraries of members of Gamaat Al-Tawhid wa Al-Jihad, whatever its connections with foreign terrorist organizations, reveal strikingly this phenomenon of radicalization of the younger generation, whose attraction to militant Islamic activism may result from a combination of socio-economic despair, identity crisis, and regional solidarity," the ICG report states. A buffer zone indeed.

Now there is talk of reviving an old Egyptian government plan to clear a "military exclusion zone" of houses and trees in the area near the Rafah border where Bedouin may smuggle but also live and farm their land. As well as winning approval from the Israelis, who complain constantly that weapons are being smuggled through tunnels under the border wall, the plan would appeal to Mubarak, who also has his own problems with the Hamas leadership on the other side of the border (Hamas originated from the Palestinian branch of the Muslim Brotherhood). The plan, locals said in July 2007, is to clear a one-hundred-and-fifty-meter-wide strip on the twelve-kilometer-long border that would later be broadened to three kilometers. Locals cite as proof of the plan the mysterious visit in July 2007 of a delegation from the U.S. Congress to inspect the area (shorthand to any Arab for attempts to strengthen Israeli border security). What is certain is that security forces are pouring into the area. They may in the short term foil some of the smuggling, but as Israeli journalist Zvi Bar'el has pointed out in *Ha'aretz,* the Bedouin "are no longer impressed by the modes of punishment at this point."

To Egypt's eternal shame—this is, after all, a country that makes it a crime to besmirch its image abroad—nearly the only help is coming from overseas. Worse, some of it comes from the U.N. World Food Program, more often associated with the victims of famine in North Korea and the displaced of sub-Saharan Africa than with booming tourist regions. Bishow Parajuli, the WFP's country director, has said: "The statistics will not show that the area is so poor." Sharm Al-Sheikh and the tourist boom "will mask that. But you need to identify the traditional communities." The WFP project in Sinai focuses on nutrition and "capacity building." But that means essentially people will be given food allowances if they agree to settle, making the program in spirit at least an arm of the Egyptian government's own policies. Its success may be measured, pace the ICG, by the fact that after five years of funding, one settlement project in central Sinai "is on the point of closure without having established the sustainable conditions for survival for the few dozen families involved." The European Commission, for its part, has awarded 55.5 million euros to a two-pronged development program in the South Sinai Governorate. The first part is infrastructure upgrades like supplying drinking water to rural communities, solid-waste and waste-water management, and environmental protection equipment for the area's nature reserves. The second part, worth 20.5 million euros, is earmarked for poverty alleviation and social development projects through local and international NGOs. According to reports, the locals are in this instance grateful—just once again not to the nation that demands their loyalty.

None of this is nearly enough to douse the powder keg that is the Sinai. As Hussein Al-Qayim, member of the pro-democracy group Kifaya, reportedly told the *Al-Ahram* newspaper after the riots in October 2007: "The government must rethink its strategy toward the Bedouin, or else those in the area who are armed will turn it into the war that Cairo seems to be pushing for."

CHAPTER FIVE

TORTURE

Abbas was staying for two weeks in my Cairo apartment, and had taken the laundry to the local dry cleaner two hours earlier. He was in his thirties and I had met him during a trip to Aswan, where he invited me to dinner at his family's home. We struck up one of those instant friendships that are common between Egyptians and foreigners, especially in the country's tourism centers, and which are as easily forged over a cup of tea as they are forgotten when each eventually goes his separate way. Abbas told me after dinner that he wanted to come to Cairo to find work. I took the hint and agreed to let him stay in the spare room in my apartment while he got on his feet. The condition was that he do the chores, which included taking the clothes to the dry cleaner. I had quickly decided that he was not entirely to be trusted since he worked in Aswan as a tout, taking from tourists a commission here and a free drink or meal there; but he was educated, witty, and generally good company, and we had the shared experience of having lived in the Saudi Arabian coastal city of Jeddah (which he loved almost as much as I did). In any case, the fifteen-hour train journey back to Cairo would be less tedious if undertaken with a companion to chat with and to smoke away the time. Now, though, as I looked out of my window to the street below to check again if he was in sight, an awful possibility flitted through my mind: This guy had taken advantage of my hospitality, stolen my clothes, and run out on me.

I reassured myself that it was a turn of events too out of the ordinary to be possible. Egyptians, despite their dire social circumstances, continue to put great store on personal character traits like honesty and dependability, and even the odd shifty individual will try to cover his tracks when getting up to no good in order to keep his social reputation intact. But he *had*, I recalled, told me he would be coming straight back; and the fact that his cell phone was switched off only increased my anxiety. I checked the apartment, finding Abbas's own clothes still there in a pile at the foot of his bed. Then again, what need would he have of them if he had stolen mine? I decided to make my way to the dry cleaner.

Mohammed, the boy at the shop, had all the answers. Yes, Abbas had dropped off the clothes, and they would be ready the following morning. But after he left, the lad continued, a policeman had called him over and asked to see his identification card. After a quick glance at it, Abbas had been told to climb into the back of a police truck. Shortly afterward, he had then been taken away with an assortment of other unfortunates—presumably to the local police station. The boy, puffing on a cigarette, was relating all this with an air of nonchalance, as though it were the most normal course of events.

"But what had he done wrong?" I wanted to know.

"Done wrong?" the boy asked in turn, with a dismissive tut and a roll of the eyes that seemed to say: You do not actually have to *do* anything in this country to get picked up by the cops.

I telephoned an acquaintance called Moussa, whose brother was a midlevel policeman, and explained what had happened. I could call in a favor from him because, at his wedding a few months earlier, I had slipped him a not inconsiderable sum of money while offering my congratulations, thinking it a wise investment in a country where who you know can get you out of all sorts of difficult situations. He told me to put on a smart shirt and tie and meet him half an hour later at the police station nearest to where Abbas had been picked up. Being white and looking official would be half the battle of getting Abbas out, he added. The other half would involve having a wad of cash on my person for liberal distribution as baksheesh. Before hanging up, he asked me for Abbas's full name and ID card number. All I knew, I admitted, was that he was called Abbas, and that he was originally from Aswan. That should do the trick, he mumbled, reasoning that it was hardly likely more than one person with that name and from that southern city had been picked up in the same Cairo district.

Moussa was waiting for me outside the police station. He had already secured the information that a vanload of "criminals" had arrived about half an hour earlier, who were now being interrogated inside. "Give me twenty pounds," he told me quietly; a little over three dollars. He walked up to the uniformed guard at the police station's entrance, shook his hand as a way of discreetly handing over the bribe folded in his palm, whispered something in the cop's ear, then gestured for me to follow him inside. A flight of stairs led up to the left, at the bottom of which stood three more uniformed cops. Moussa took another wad of notes from me, introduced himself to the cops as the brother of an officer, and again was granted safe passage. At the top of the stairs yet more baksheesh opened the door to the grubby office of a more senior officer, whom Moussa engaged in conversation as I waited outside. He returned, told me to give him whatever money I still had on me (about forty dollars), and suggested it would be best if I went back down to the street. Ten minutes later, Abbas emerged from the police station. Moussa was with him, an arm flung over Abbas's shoulder. Abbas greeted me with hugs and kisses. We hailed the first taxi and sped off to my apartment, after I had reassured Moussa that I would "see him later" in order to give him—he was supposed to understand—a thank-you for his services. I would have paid him there and then, but all I had left of the money I had brought with me was a battered ten pound note and I needed that for the taxi fare.

"Why did they pick you up?" I asked Abbas when we were back in the apartment.

"They do this all the time," he replied. "They have a quota system. They just pick up twenty or thirty guys from the street every day, and then they frisk you inside the police station to see if you have any drugs or anything else illegal on you. If you don't have anything, you wait for them to check your file on the computer, to see if there are any outstanding warrants for your arrest. If there aren't any, they let you go."

So if I had just left him there, would he have been released anyway?

"It can take a day or two," he explained. "In the meantime, you're not allowed to call anyone to let them know where you are or what's happening. And you are thrown into a little room with so many others. The officer is happy just to get lucky with two or three arrests a day from the dozens he picks up. Then he can tell his boss he's fulfilled his quota for arresting criminals."

"But that's ridiculous," I protested. "Cops are supposed to look for criminals who are suspected of having committed reported crimes, not arrest all and sundry in the hope that one or two of them might have done something wrong. Why didn't you just refuse to go with them? They have no right to do this."

He looked at me as though I were a fool.

"They have the right to do whatever they want," he said. "You should understand by now that in this country the people have no rights anymore. If you protest, they take you downstairs and beat the shit out of you."

He was quiet for a moment, as though reflecting on something he had witnessed earlier in the day.

"Fuck this country, and fuck this government," he finally spat out. "I want to leave. I don't care where to. Any country is better than this one."

Abbas was actually fortunate in a number of ways, most obviously in that he knew a Westerner who himself had connections to intervene and obtain his release. But more important was that he understood the system well enough to stoically accept his fate and not object, knowing that to do so would only result in worse punishment than the rather arbitrary inconvenience to which he was being subjected. Too many others in Egypt are not so lucky, as the arbitrariness of the regime's thugs—bored, underpaid, intimidated themselves—too often results in violence for the sake of violence, all part of a system that sees routine intimidation as central to an ability to rule.

For example: Mohammed Abdul Rahman was born into an impoverished family in the village of Shouha in the Nile Delta. He was thirteen years old when he became an enemy of the Egyptian state, and as a result would not live to see his fourteenth birthday. It is alleged that in August 2007 he was arrested along with his older adolescent brother, Ibrahim. His alleged crime? Police in the nearby city of Mansoura suspected that the pair had stolen packets of tea. When their mother visited them three days later at Mansoura Police Station, after finally getting word of their whereabouts, she has said she was "shocked to death" at the sight of Mohammed.

But she said nothing at the police station itself. This was to spare the older son from further persecution at the hands of his tormentors. She rushed from the police station to a lawyer. He managed to get little Mohammed transferred to a Mansoura public hospital.

For Egypt's impoverished masses, alas, being transferred from a police station to a chronically underfunded public hospital means being thrown from the frying pan into the fire. That was what it must have seemed like to Mohammed, who was said to have spent four days there—that is, assuming he was able to think about anything other than the excruciating pain he was in. On the fifth day, Mohammed was handed back to the police by locals who found him lying unconscious in a parking lot near the hospital. His mother accused the hospital of, literally, throwing him away and not caring for him, though it is impossible to know how he got to the parking lot. According to reports, the police, unable to inflict more cruelty on a child already at the point of death, finally decided they had had enough of him. They took him back home to his mother, which of course is what you would expect to be done with a thirteen year old on the day of his arrest.

As in so many other instances of police brutality in Egypt, that might have been the end of the story. At least for everyone but the boy's family. But the case came to the attention of the Muslim Brotherhood. They visited the family's ramshackle hut, video camera at the ready. In the resulting video clip the mother, wearing a simple peasant head scarf, can be seen telling her story. Mohammed lies semiconscious on a mattress behind her. His mouth is open, his breathing labored. At the request of the interviewer, she whips off the sheet covering her son. Revealed is his desperately thin body, a fluid shunt attached to his lung. She points out several burn marks on his front before turning the moaning child over to reveal a huge black mark on his back. She says it became infected following his treatment. The camera zooms in on the mark. Then it travels downward, to the little boy's anus. It looks slack and distended—as if he had recently been raped. Again, the boy is turned over. Now the mother points to more burn marks on his penis and testicles.

Mohammed Abdul Rahman was never again to regain full consciousness, and a few days after the video was shot he died.

Magda Adly, the director of the Al-Nadim Center for the Psychological Treatment and Rehabilitation of the Victims of Violence, later said that Mohammed's family told her he had both electrical burns and burns that seemed to come from a heated object. His brother said Mohammed had been tortured with a heating coil. "The boy was beaten, electrocuted. When he screamed and went into convulsions, the officer kicked him in the chest, and that appears to have damaged his lungs," Adly concluded. The coma, she said, could have been caused either by blood poisoning or head trauma from the terrible beatings he must have endured.

His mother told reporters that the doctors who initially examined the body to issue the death certificate also suspected he died of unnatural causes and advised her to go to a prosecutor. One prosecutor wept when he saw the body, she added; and he had it transferred to the Mansoura University Hospital morgue. A preliminary autopsy showed the direct cause of death was pulmonary infection. That may indeed have been true. However, the question the mother said she wanted answered by the doctors was what brought it on. She said she refused to accept the autopsy result or to have the body released for burial. Senior local officials and policemen then "tried to bribe me and other times to threaten me so as not to file a complaint," she alleged, offering her two hundred dollars—a large sum for a poor, illiterate head of a large family. But it was not enough to persuade this proud, heartbroken woman to let the matter rest.

Tired of the negotiations, it is alleged police then simply whisked the body away from the morgue without telling the mother. They buried the boy, apparently while her other son Ibrahim, who was still in custody, was sitting in the back of a police pickup truck looking on. Was this an implicit warning to him to tell his mother to shut up or he, too, would be killed?

Ibrahim, meanwhile, was also claiming that he had been tortured by police, who threatened to fabricate a drug charge against him unless he testified that the burn marks on his brother's body were the lingering effect of a live electric cable that just happened to fall on him six months before he was detained. Thinking Mohammed was still alive, Ibrahim agreed. But by the time of the burial, the Muslim Brotherhood had posted the video on their Web site, and the case was attracting enormous publicity—not just in the Egyptian opposition media, which routinely exposes alleged torture cases in graphic detail, but also briefly in the usually uninterested international media. Ibrahim retracted his testimony and the prosecutor-general's office, in a departure from practice, announced it would investigate the case further. It exhumed Mohammed's body for more testing. Hamdi Al-Baz, the family's lawyer, said there were "clear circumstances here calling for the body to be reexamined," and cited a report made by the health inspector while the boy was first hospitalized which said torture was involved. Al-Baz added that one had only to look at the speed with which the body was taken away for burial to see that the Interior Ministry wanted to end the matter quickly. "There is a web of conspiracy here . . . all in an attempt to hide the true circumstances of his death," he was quoted by opposition newspapers as saying. Al-Baz then prepared a case file, including the video that had by then been watched on the Web by tens of thousands around the world.

Egyptian justice is nothing if not swift.

By early September, a government-appointed panel of forensic experts completely cleared the Mansoura police officers of all charges. It found that the boy had died due to "a sharp drop in blood pressure and respiratory functions." Of course that finding is completely consistent with the family's story also.

Such a reputation do police stations have among ordinary Egyptians that these days they are loath to report even serious crimes, lest they get on the wrong side of a surly officer or, worse, are found to be filing a complaint against someone who has "connections" and who can then make the claimants' lives a living hell by placing a few calls to influential individuals in power. Women who are victims of sexual violence especially almost never report the crimes, women's rights organizations have said. You do not have to look very hard to discover why. Since the officers themselves routinely employ rape as an interrogation technique or perhaps just for fun (even, it is alleged, with a frail, thirteen-year-old boy like Mohammed, merely accused of stealing a packet of tea), they unsurprisingly turn out to be far from sympathetic listeners; add to this the lingering belief in this male-chauvinist society that women who are raped somehow were asking for it, and the inapproachability becomes absolute. Women who nevertheless have braved the intimidation at the all-male police stations have said the experience merely added insult to injury. They report that the first reaction of a thug they encounter, who calls himself an officer, is a snide remark along the lines of whether she would perhaps like to "meet up" later that evening at a fast-food restaurant to discuss the issue further. Her "honor" no longer intact, she is to blame; and so she is now considered fair game.

One is at a loss at what to say in such a context in response to the arrest in 2001 by several hundred security personnel of a few dozen presumed "homosexuals" dancing on a cruise boat moored on the Nile in Cairo. The fifty-two detained men (thirty-five arrested on the boat and seventeen from other areas of Cairo) were, reports claim, subjected to torture, and some were severely beaten. Even the youngest, only fifteen and not at the disco when he was arrested, told journalists he had been beaten with a *falaka*—a thick stick—across the legs and feet. This instrument of torture frequently leaves its victims unable to walk for days. The trial itself was sheer pandemonium, as families and relatives were denied entrance to the court and the morale of the prisoners slumped as they discovered they were to be tried before a State Security Court (originally set up to deal with cases of terrorism and espionage) with no right of appeal. State-sponsored thugs, who are alleged to routinely employ anal rape as a form of torture against male detainees, arresting a group of men merely because they were dancing together: it goes well beyond irony. It points, in fact, to the rank hypocrisy and cold brutality at the heart of the Mubarak regime, and a country where the security services exist not to protect the people from crime but to protect the leaders of the country from the people who despise them.

The video clip of Mohammed brought home to tens of thousands of Internet surfers the world over, and those who read the occasional report on the subject reprinted in the Western media, what every Egyptian has known for years: Torture is rife in their country's security system. Indeed, this was not even the first time it had been captured on video for all the world to see. In a clip taken with a camera phone that appeared the previous November on an Egyptian blog, police officers were seen sodomizing a prisoner (apprehended after daring to challenge the arrest of his brother) with a broomstick—a practice, according to an extensive Amnesty International report on torture in Egypt, that is routine. "Torture and other forms of ill-treatment are systematic in detention centers," the report concludes. Local lobbying groups concur. The Egyptian Organization for Human Rights (EOHR), for example, published a report in 2007 detailing hundreds of victims of police brutality over the previous decade. "Torture in Egypt is methodical and systematic, unlike what the Interior Ministry would have you believe," stated Tariq Zaghloul, EOHR's director of field operations, adding: "It is not individual cases." The organization's report says that torture is a phenomenon in Egypt buttressed by lenient legal procedures that allow the practice to flourish. Between 1993 and July 2007, EOHR documented over five hundred people who had been tortured. Of the 567 victims, 167 died as a direct result of police actions, the organization stated. And these cases, presumably, represent only the tip of the iceberg, since most are hushed up before they can see the light of day.

What is well known is that the most frequently reported methods of torture are beatings, electric shocks, suspension by the wrists and ankles and in contorted positions for long periods, and threats that the victims or their relatives would be killed, raped, or otherwise sexually abused. Some detainees have told Amnesty International they were interrogated while fellow inmates were being tortured nearby, suggesting that there is a kind of twenty-four-hour conveyor belt. Others said they heard the screams of people being tortured and saw the injuries of prisoners after they had been interrogated. Of the people detained in connection with terrorist attacks in Taba in 2004 and Sharm Al-Sheikh in 2005, many said that their hands were tied and that they were stripped naked and blindfolded throughout the sessions. One former "terrorist suspect" detainee, Ahmed Abdallah

Rabaa, said he was interrogated and tortured three to four times a day—beaten, suspended by the ankles and wrists in contorted positions, and given electric shocks to sensitive parts of the body, including his lips, penis, and head. Each time he was interrogated and tortured, he was blindfolded and made to take off all his clothes. Unlike in Mohammed's case, however, a doctor came almost every day to check on the torture victims, to make sure that their ordeal could continue. It appears that Rabaa was tortured thus during nearly three months' detention, either because his brother was a terrorist suspect or—and this is not a joke—because of a mix-up in names.

Typically, detainees of the Egyptian state security forces are held incommunicado or in secret. In other words, in the time-honored fashion of military dictatorships everywhere, they are "disappeared." In general, the only detainees who are told the reason for their incarceration are those arrested simply because they are related to a suspect. In some cases, these relatives are then released but told that they should find the wanted people and convince them to surrender to the authorities to stop the torture or other ill-treatment of yet other relatives still in detention—hence the fear of the mother of little Mohammed about speaking out while both her sons were still in detention. The practice is eerily similar to what in Nazi Germany was known as *Sippenhaft,* "a very old custom practiced among our forefathers," as Himmler himself put it in 1944.

One victim, a twenty-two-year-old university student, can stand for many in that he was never charged, his allegations of torture were never investigated, and of course he received no reparation for his suffering. He told Amnesty International that he was arrested at around three o'clock in the morning at his home, blindfolded, and taken to a State Security Investigations (SSI) services office in Al-Arish on the Sinai peninsula. He was asked to identify certain people, but when he said he had no idea who they were, he was insulted and repeatedly punched in the face. His interrogators then stripped him naked, tied his hands behind his back, bound his feet together, and suspended him by the wrists from the top of an open door. One wire was attached to one of his toes and the other to his penis, and he was given electric shocks. He had water poured on his face, and was made to lie on the floor. All this happened while he was naked and blindfolded. The same kind of torture continued for a week. Sometimes he was also forced to be present while other detainees were being interrogated and tortured; at other times he could hear the screams of fellow detainees. He spent fourteen days in the SSI office in Al-Arish before being transferred to a Central Security Forces detention center.

All the available evidence suggests that attempts by the regime at combating routine torture amounts to little more than window dressing. In November 2007, for instance, just days after two police officers were sentenced to three years in prison for sodomizing a man with a stick in the case mentioned above, another man died from his injuries after being tortured by Egyptian police for three days. Egyptian officials told foreign news agencies that Ahmed Saber Saad had been held on suspicion of drug possession, but although state prosecutors ordered his release on the grounds that there was insufficient evidence against him, police instead tortured Saad for three days before dumping him on the street. He died a day later. The Egyptian Prosecutor General Abdel Meguid Mahmoud ordered an inquiry into the reports, but before the investigation had even gotten underway two other police officers were put "under investigation" after two adolescent boys alleged that they ordered other prisoners to rape them at another police station. A lieutenant and first lieutenant at the Kafr Al-Sheikh station in Cairo allegedly ordered older prisoners to rape the boys, ages sixteen and seventeen, after the two were arrested for drug possession a week earlier and ordered detained for four days. After their release, the teenagers' families filed a complaint with the local prosecutor's office, and a forensic examination taken after they left police custody reportedly showed they had recently been sodomized. The Interior Ministry released a statement saying the police director of the Kafr Al-Sheikh station, a police general, and two of his senior assistants were removed from their posts and transferred to "administrative jobs."

If all this sounds strangely familiar—the nakedness, the blindfolding, the suspension—it is because it came before the public eye in a different country and administered by a different torture master, namely in Baghdad's Abu Ghraib prison in the early days of the Iraq invasion. Already on September 26, 2001, before any "war on terror" had fully taken shape, then U.S. Secretary of State Colin Powell was loud in his "appreciation for the commitment that Egypt has made to working with us as we move forward to deal with the scourge of terrorism. Egypt, as all of us know, is really ahead of us on this issue. And we have much to learn from them and there is much we can do together." One of the things the two allies were able to do together before long was interrogate prisoners; they did this under the U.S. system of "extraordinary rendition"—a term coined to mean secretly spiriting detainees from U.S. and other jurisdictions to a country where law and law enforcement are less ostensibly scrupulous about using torture to extract information. Besides Saudi Arabia, Egypt was to prove a prime candidate for such cooperative efforts.

When Egyptian authorities consider that a case in any way affects national security, they have a hundred legal ways to circumvent guarantees to a fair trial, the right to legal counsel, the obligation to investigate allegations of torture and other ill-treatment, and the ban on using evidence extracted under torture in court. National security cases are dealt with by what human rights campaigners say is effectively a whole "parallel legal system" that can deprive the accused of a right to equality before the law from prosecution to trial. Cases deemed to be security-related are investigated by a special branch of the Public Prosecution—the Supreme State Security Prosecution—or are referred to the Supreme Military Prosecution by the president. Defendants are then tried, not before the normal courts but before emergency or military courts, which are bound by few inconvenient safeguards (including the right of appeal to a higher tribunal). In principle, the prosecution conducts a criminal case by investigating offenses either through law enforcement officers or by delegating the task to an examining magistrate, but that is entirely at the discretion of the Public Prosecution. In security cases, prosecutors can simply decide to conduct the investigation themselves, using the Supreme State Security Prosecution, which specializes in such offences and is directly supervised by the public prosecutor. Since a year after the 1952 coup, when the Supreme State Security Prosecution was established, its powers have been expanded by other decrees. Now members can investigate security offenses anywhere in Egypt, plus any crimes the president sees fit to refer to it. And they, of course, are legion.

The emergency law of 1952 also gives the Public Prosecution the powers of an examining magistrate and of an appeals court of trials in camera. And it gives sweeping powers to the public prosecutor to hold people suspected of terrorist offenses. All this combined means he can first order a pretrial detention for fifteen days in his capacity as a public prosecutor; then he can extend the detention for up to forty-five days wearing the hat of an examining magistrate; and stepping nimbly into the shoes of an accusation appeals chamber, he can then keep renewing the detention for periods of fifteen days. In other words, the public prosecutor has the power to detain people for up to five months without independent judicial oversight. During the first fifteen days, anyone can be deprived of their right to be brought promptly before a judge or other judicial officer and is denied the right even to challenge their detention, however unlikely success may be when they finally do get the opportunity. Almost needless to add, responsibility for investigating allegations of torture during detention then lies . . . with the public prosecutor.

America's web of extraordinary renditions took advantage of the black hole the Egyptian system creates by choosing victims who were mostly Egyptian nationals and Egyptians with dual nationality, who can therefore conceivably be said to come under their native country's jurisdiction and to be endangering its security (if they endangered anyone's). The CIA's rendition flights, by way of European and Pakistani airports, are a matter of record. Nobody knows how many people were thus "rendered" like fat off a carcass, but most of those who were later able to speak out about their experiences were handcuffed and blindfolded on arrival at Cairo airport and then whisked off to a secret detention facility that is apparently run by the General Intelligence.

One of them was Mamdouh Habib, an Egyptian with an Australian passport. His case gained widespread media attention, and many of the facts are well established. On October 5, 2001, he was arrested in Pakistan, where he alleges he was beaten and threatened for nearly a month to get him to sign a confession. When that proved futile, he was handed over to what he said were about fifteen U.S. officials, stripped of his clothes, photographed, sedated, and flown to Egypt. During the flight, he said, Egyptian security officers deprived him of sleep. On arrival at Cairo airport, he says he was handcuffed, blindfolded, and taken to a building surrounded by high walls. He recalls that the car drove for about ten to fifteen minutes before it descended into what appeared to be an underground location in the building. He was stripped of his clothes, photographed, and put in a room, where a doctor checked his heart. He was then visited by two Egyptian security officers and asked to cooperate and confess that he was planning to hijack a plane to commit terrorist acts. When he refused, he says he was drugged and put in a tiny cell with a dim amber light and a hole in the ceiling. During interrogation, he said, he was hung from hooks in the ceiling, beaten, given electric shocks, and threatened with rape and death and the death of his relatives. He was also, he claims, forced into torture chambers, one of which was filled with water so high that he had to stand on tiptoe for hours in order not to drown. Another chamber had a very low ceiling and held two feet of water, forcing him to maintain a painful stoop. Yet another had a few inches of water and an electric generator, which he was told would electrocute him. Under such alleged conditions, he confessed that he helped train the September 11 attackers in martial arts. He later withdrew the confession. Habib told anyone who would listen to his story that the systematic use of drugs and electric shocks temporarily paralyzed the left side of his body. He was bleeding from his eyes and ears and often pissed blood. When his health got worse, he was taken to a room on a higher floor where he was seen regularly by a doctor, apparently to treat him before his release. He was then told by the security officers that he was no longer needed in Egypt. Early one morning, he reports he was blindfolded, chained, had his mouth and eyes covered with tape, and was put in a van that took him to the airport. In a second van at the airport, a security officer filmed Habib—again the Abu Ghraib echo—as he was stripped, had the tape removed from his face and mouth, and was photographed before being blindfolded and gagged yet again and put on a plane to Afghanistan. From there he was taken to Guantánamo Bay—a facility on nobody's soil that is even farther beyond the reach of the law than Egypt, but inconvenienced by occasional media attention—where he was held for nearly another three years. Finally, he was released without charge.

Perhaps the most famous victim of extraordinary rendition is the Egyptian known as Abu Omar, a radical Islamist who was abducted in February 2003 by CIA agents in a spy-movie-style operation involving the inevitable white van and a location as close as it is possible to get to the heart of Western civilization: Milan. He was, it is alleged, spirited to Egypt on a CIA-chartered plane and handed over to the secret services, who held him incommunicado for fourteen months before releasing him on the promise that he would tell no one what had been done to him. Twenty-three days later he claims he was arrested again, because he had told relatives about his ordeal over the phone. On arrival in Cairo, he says he suffered the whole mindless catalog of humiliations—stripping, being photographed, hooding—before being taken to the General Intelligence headquarters, where he was kept for seven months, apparently because he refused to work as an informant in Italy. He was then transferred to SSI offices for a further seven months, where he says he was also tortured. "I was exposed to all forms of crucifixion. They crucified me on a metal door, and on a wooden apparatus which they call Al-Arousa or 'the bride,' hands up high, behind my back, to the sides as well as the feet tightly together and spread apart, and tortured me during crucifixion by means of electric shocks and by kicking and beating with electric cables and water hoses and whipping," Abu Omar said in a letter he later smuggled out of jail. The second inventive method he said he was subjected to was what is called "the mattress." "It is a mattress that is placed on the tiled floor of the torture chamber and it is wet down with water and attached to electricity," he wrote. "My hands were tied behind my back and so were my feet; and someone sat on a wooden chair between my shoulder blades and another sat on a wooden chair between my legs, and the electricity was switched on; and I find my-self raised from the strength of the electricity that is touching the water, but the wooden chairs are keeping me from rising higher, and then the electricity is switched off and the interrogator tortures me by electric shocks to my genitals while cursing me and yelling, 'Let Italy be of benefit to you.'" Presumably the mockery was directed at any belief Abu Omar may have had that he would be protected by Italian law.

Like all repressive regimes in the Arab world, Egypt knows that con-tributing to America's "war on terror" will limit criticism from Washington about its own human rights abuses while justifying repressive measures against the masses at home. Thus it came as little surprise when, in Decem-ber 2007, a U.S.-based human rights group accused the Egyptian govern-ment of using torture and false confessions in a high-profile antiterrorism case, where twenty-two alleged members of an unknown Islamist group, the Victorious Sect, were accused of planning attacks on tourism sites and gas pipelines. Human Rights Watch said its research suggests the security forces may have fabricated the group's name and that the allegations were basically made up in order to justify renewing emergency laws. Although the state prosecutor himself dismissed the charges against the suspects, ten of them are still believed to be in detention.

One curious point that emerges from these allegations is a strange, twisted respect among the torturers for legal process. For besides laboriously em-powering prosecutors to act with impunity within its confines, Egyptian law also defines torture quite narrowly only in the context of forcing an ac-cused to confess; the result is that only some of the practices banned inter-nationally are prohibited under Egyptian law. Death threats and physical torture are actually criminalized only when they happen after an unlawful arrest by someone purporting to be a government officer. The law in any case does not deal with torture for other reasons—to extract information, intimidate, punish, or degrade—or when the victim is not accused of an offense. And indeed it appears the torturers, mindful of the law, rarely use torture to extract confessions—except with extraordinarily rendered suspects, where U.S. encouragement acts as a kind of divine sanction—but they use it liberally to get their victims to incriminate others or yield up information, as they apparently did with little Mohammed's brother, or for no particular reason at all.

The torture practices security officers use are of course as ingenious as they have been from time immemorial, and the global economy is a friendly environment in which they can thrive, providing them with all the tools they need and more. "Torture implements are produced—mostly in the West—and sold openly, frequently to nasty regimes in developing countries and even through the Internet," the contrary Israeli columnist Sam Vaknin has written. "Hi-tech devices abound: sophisticated electro-convulsive stun guns, painful restraints, truth serums, chemicals such as pepper gas. Export licensing is universally minimal and nonintrusive and completely ignores the technical specifications of the goods (for instance, whether they could be lethal or merely inflict pain)." Amnesty International and the U.K.-based Omega Foundation have found more than one hundred and fifty manufacturers of stun guns in the United States. They face tough competition from Germany (thirty companies), Taiwan (nineteen), France (fourteen), South Korea (thirteen), China (twelve), South Africa (nine), Israel (eight), Mexico (six), Poland (four), Russia (four), Brazil (three), Spain (three), and the Czech Republic (two). American high-voltage electroshock stun shields have turned up in Turkey, stun guns in Indonesia, and electroshock batons and shields and dart-firing Taser guns in Saudi Arabia. American firms are also the dominant manufacturers of so-called stun belts. Amnesty International quotes Dennis Kaufman, the president of Stun Tech Inc., an American manufacturer, as saying: "Electricity speaks every language known to man. No translation necessary. Everybody is afraid of electricity, and rightfully so." Kaufman insists that his products are not designed for torture, but for temporary incapacitation without harm. According to Amnesty, the European Commission, meanwhile, at one stage gave a quality award to a Taiwanese manufacturer of electric batons but, when challenged, could not cite evidence of independent safety tests for the baton or whether member states of the European Union had even been consulted on the issue.

But the greatest contribution of our time, as Abu Ghraib made clear, has been the stress on deliberate humiliation, and especially sexual humiliation—for men, that is (women have always been so treated). "The worst thing that happened to me was taking my clothes off because it affects my psychology," the twenty-two-year-old student quoted by Amnesty International said. And Abu Omar claimed: "I was sexually abused and sodomized twice, and this was the worst thing that I went through. For signs of physical torture eventually go away, and the pain goes away, but the psychological repercussions and the bitterness and scandal of sexual violation remain. This sexual violation occurred twice, where my hands were restrained behind my back and so were my feet, and they laid me on my stomach, naked, and someone lay on top of me and began to try to rape me, and I screamed so hard and so loud that I passed out, and I don't know whether he raped me or he was just intimidating and threatening." If the last sentence sounds like an afterthought—notice that he goes from "this sexual violation occurred" to "I don't know whether he raped me"—it only enforces the point that sexual humiliation is the most potent means of breaking down victims through their shame, be they Arab victims or any other. The outcry in the Arab world over the torture pictures from Abu Ghraib also focused obsessively on the sexual violations or, to be more exact, on the same-sex simulations the prisoners were forced into. And that is especially hurtful, and so especially effective as a torture tool, because homosexuality is taboo in the Arab and wider Islamic world. However, not only is it a natural outlet in cultures that enforce varying degrees of segregation of the sexes, but it is also a rich tradition in the Middle East, yet due to an equal and opposite obsession with masculinity and manly honor it is not usually openly acknowledged.

I asked myself a question as I stood in traffic-choked Lazoghly Square in southern Cairo, looking up at the black marble arch that looms like an all-too-neat symbol of brute state power over the entrance to Interior Ministry headquarters, the *Lubyanka* of the Egyptian security services: What is the point of all this torture? I mean, what use is it? After all, Abu Omar, like so many others, was eventually let go without charge: In February 2007, four years almost to the day after it was alleged CIA agents first bundled him into their van, he was simply put out into the street.

At the time of my visit to Lazoghly Square in mid-2007, another video clip that had been posted on YouTube was fresh in my mind. Of a smeary, grainy appearance suggesting it was taken with a camera phone, it shows a policeman, strapping in his all-white uniform like a steward on a cruise liner, beating up a group of what appear to be freshly arrested civilians in a police station. The first two victims, both at least a head shorter than the policeman and wrapped in peasant scarves, stand facing the wall, cowering and trying to protect their heads with their hands and pleading for mercy. The officer keeps ordering them to face the wall and repeatedly adjusts their stance, grabbing them by the scruffs of their necks, banging their foreheads into the wall and shaking them into position while he hollers at them. He is light on his feet but strangely jerky in his movements, like an exotic forest bird at its mating dance. As he trips around the victims, he keeps his right hand raised at a stiff right angle and again and again brings the tensed side of his palm bouncing down on the back of their necks in a sort of inept karate chop. There is something listless about the performance, something bored as well as compulsive, as if he is at a loss as to what to do with all this power he must exercise. The camera at one point pulls back to reveal several more prisoners waiting in line, who are pushed forward by someone outside the frame to endure the same ministrations. The officer duly bangs them into the wall and chops at their necks a few times, but already his attention is wandering. Presently, from somewhere, he acquires a rubber baton, whose intermittent thwacks off camera, followed by the groans of other victims, we realize we have been hearing all along. This briefly renews his interest as he brings it down hard on the first two prisoners' thighs; but he is essentially spent, there is nothing else he can think to do, so he turns to camera with a wide grin on his handsome face, spreads his hands as if to say, "And this is how we deal with enemies of the state," and the clip ends.

At only two minutes and thirty-three seconds, the clip makes for dull viewing. I had been tempted to turn it off, not so much because I could bear no more of the violence but because, shamefully, I had been expecting something more revealing than this repetitive pointlessness. Now I realized that my feelings perhaps provided a clue to the problem of torture in Egypt, as it was to manifest itself, for example, in little Mohammed's case, whose video had caused me nightmares after I read that he had died. Why, I kept asking myself, did the Brothers not take him to their best hospital, where at least he might have stood a chance? For policemen, however brutal, to electrocute, burn, and rape a thirteen-year-old boy to death for allegedly stealing a packet of tea, they have to be bored out of their minds with the routine abuse and violence they dole out to adult victims over more serious infractions. This suggested that torture must have been endemic for a very long time, surrounded by a culture of impunity carefully buttressed by the emergency law, and so entrenched that it was now wholly separated from any law-enforcement purposes it may once have had, to become an end in itself. In our entrepreneurial climate, it is unfashionable to blame the system; and of course the main reason for torture in Egypt is to further intimidate the oppressed masses. But studies of genocide, for example, show again and again that perfectly decent people can turn into killers if the system provides an environment of impunity, and that they become bolder and more adventurous in their killings the longer they are so empowered. This is precisely what the Egyptian state has done for torture.

The Egyptian annual budget for internal security in 2006 was $1.5 billion, more than the entire national budget for health care, and there are estimated to be 1.4 million security officers, a cadre nearly four times the size of the army. The Egyptian Organization for Human Rights found that while the population of the country nearly doubled during the first twenty-five years of Mubarak's regime, the number of prisons grew more than fourfold, and the number of detainees held for more than one year without charge or indictment grew to more than twenty thousand. Egypt, in the words of Ibrahim Eissa, the fiery editor of the opposition *Al-Dostour* newspaper, "has become a police state par excellence." In the course of the soul searching in the Egyptian press that followed little Mohammed's death, others also pointed to a sickness at the heart of the system. Ahmed Hegazi, from the Arab Organization for Human Rights in Cairo, told *Al-Ahram Weekly* the problem began with the training of young police cadets. "Much of the training is military in style and concentrates on building physical strength," he said. Actual police work, he added, is barely taught, and the methods are usually outdated, so police officers soon learn that exerting a little physical pressure on a prisoner can yield quicker results than proper investigation. And from a handful of highly publicized cases, they learn that even a death in custody is unlikely to lead to any repercussions. Meanwhile, Mubarak's hold on power is slipping, and that perhaps adds whatever impetus may still have been lacking to crack down harder and harder on threats to the regime or, more likely, to try to cow the population by setting ever more brutal examples. Then again, as with the sort of press reports saying that deaths from smoking are "on the rise," it is difficult to tell whether the perceived increase in police brutality is simply due to an increase in perception or coverage. Ultimately, as with much else that is wrong with Egypt, Nasser is to blame, having set up the torture centers officially known as prisons so brutal that they were referred to by their tens of thousands of inmates as "concentration camps."

Proper police work has long gone out the window completely if the investigation into the notorious December 2005 killing known as the Beni Mazar massacre is anything to go by. The hackneyed farce of rounding and roughing up the usual suspects remains such an easily available alternative. In the Beni Mazar case, which occupied the front pages of the newspapers for months, four men, two women, and four children—the eldest only eleven years old—were ritually butchered on December 29, 2005, in Beni Mazar, 225 kilometers south of Cairo. When they were discovered, the victims were in a stage of recent rigor mortis, the faded blood-splatter patterns indicating that they had bled to death. The bodies had cuts on their heads and throats and the stomachs had been slashed. In the case of the males, both the adults and the children had had their genitalia cut off. The women had their stomachs slashed open all the way back to the top of the rectum. Some of the victims had defensive cuts on their hands, but police determined that the lone deranged giant who had overpowered all eleven of them was a neighbor of below-average intelligence named Mohammed Ali, who had apparently once made a nuisance of himself on the family's roof, but who betrayed otherwise no signs of a psychotic personality. The only time he became agitated under independent psychological observation later was when he was told that police wanted to ask him more questions. For once, however, things did not go the prosecutor's way. Ali's trial in July 2006 instead brought to light the sheer incompetence of the police frame-up, which had been more like an X-rated version of the Keystone Cops than a conspiracy deserving of the name.

Despite the magnitude of the case, for example, the police had brought no fingerprint expert to the scene, arguing in court that the mud bricks of the building where the victims were killed would not have shown any prints anyway. Ali had then allegedly led police to the place where he had hidden the body parts of his victims before he had gone home—forgetting, incidentally, to wash out the *galabiya* he had allegedly worn for the deed and which, experts mobilized by the defense said, showed minimal blood splatter, which was inconsistent with the butchering of nearly a dozen people. And the genitals of the victims were where he said they would be, suggesting that they had simply been planted there by Ali following instructions by the police. Defense lawyers added that according to the prosecutor's report the crime was not reenacted by the accused, as is customary, but by someone else because Ali was "tired." In court, Ali was asked to try on a shoe that had been admitted into evidence, having allegedly been found at his home and somehow later linked to the crime. When he did, it did not fit. After three attempts, the shoes he was wearing in court were examined. They were a size forty-five, whereas the size of the shoe presented as evidence was a size forty-two. The following day, however, when an expert was called in, the shoe did magically fit the defendant. There were other holes in the case, including contradictory forensic reports and witness testimony, highlighted by Ali's defense team, which was led by member of parliament for Menoufiya Talaat Al-Sadat, who had been instrumental in getting the case reexamined by independent academics. Al-Sadat said the police were "only interested in filling the blanks, instead of doing real investigative work." All this proved too much even for the Egyptian justice system, and the court cleared Ali of all charges.

Of course, Ali (it was claimed) had been tortured into an early confession, and so had his family. Ali's father said he could hear his son scream from the pain of electric shocks he was subjected to while being interrogated. Apparently out of petty spite, police after the verdict rounded up about thirty members of Ali's family and made them sit on the floor for hours in a police station, ostensibly to shield them from a mob attack after the Interior Ministry incited the families of the victims against Ali. Susan Fayad, a psychologist from the Nadim Center, which was crucial in undermining the evidence in Ali's case, said it was "a little protection mixed in with a little punishment." They were later kept under house arrest for their "protection" and their mobile phones confiscated. Fayad, who had worked with numerous victims of violence, said the case highlighted how routine torture is.

It would be tempting to conclude that Ali's acquittal shows that the system has not completely failed. But not very much, as it happens, since his defense lawyer, Al-Sadat, was himself sentenced under a different case to a year in jail, in November 2006, for that gravest of crimes: "insulting the army." It is difficult not to believe that this was in some way payback for his exposure of their criminality and brutality, not to mention utter lack of even superficial credibility, in helping Ali to get an innocent verdict.

A deeper and more troubling explanation of the acceptance of torture was suggested from faraway Kuwait, prompted by news in August 2007 of the alleged torture of two Egyptians by Kuwaiti immigration police not long after little Mohammed died. "In the Middle East today, torture is a way of life," *Kuwait Times* staff writer Rania El-Gamal, herself an Egyptian, wrote in a powerful response to the allegations. "It is everywhere, inside our homes; parents beat and sometimes kill their children if they misbehave or 'dishonor' the family. In the workplace, stories abound of employers who abuse and torture their maids or drivers. In some schools in the Arab world, beating a child is the duty of the teacher with the blessing of parents. And don't forget police stations and prisons, where human dignity is long forgotten and human rights are a joke." The response of most Arabs to such news, she says, is at best a shrug or a sarcastic "Welcome to the Middle East." From birth, she continues, "we are taught that we should always agree and follow, never argue and disagree. Agree with our parents, our elders, our teachers, our government, our employers; just say yes to be able to live comfortably. Follow the good example of others, follow what others say or do; just follow others—as long it will keep you out of trouble. We are taught that disobeying has regretful and sometimes disastrous consequences. We are never taught to be heroes. We are just taught to be sheep who follow the shepherd and his dogs." El-Gamal has no time for people who say the fact that such torture is exposed and investigated in Kuwait means its democracy works better than Egypt's. "Is that our best reaction?" she demands. "It doesn't matter whether there is true democracy or not: We should condemn, not find a reason for a crime. We should be courageous enough to stand against what's wrong, and not be swept along with others as long as no one is looking and everyone else is doing the same. We should stop being sheep, because one day or another, we will be slaughtered."

El-Gamal, in this harsh assessment, makes two related and very valid points: Abuse has become an integral part of the fabric of Middle Eastern culture and is no longer limited to its freak show of geriatric regimes; and this has made the individuals within it complicit in the abuse their regimes mete out—made each of them, in fact, the reason the regimes continue to do so with impunity. Contrast the extraordinary outpouring of sympathy on the day of the execution of the Arab world's worst-ever butcher, Saddam Hussein, throughout Egypt and the wider Middle East, to the shedding of not a single tear for his hundreds of thousands of victims. The sickness, in other words, runs not just through the system but through the whole of society, to the point where it perhaps no longer matters who infected whom. A matter often skirted in polite conversation about oppressive regimes in the developing world is that the perpetrators, too, are "somebody's husband, somebody's son," in Gordon Burn's memorable phrase about the Yorkshire Ripper, an infamous British serial killer. In the case of Egypt's superarmy of 1.4 million police, this is a hardly insignificant minority of underpaid men who, with few other avenues of earning a living open to them, struggle amid mass unemployment and poverty to make ends meet and support a family to whom they are no doubt dutiful husbands and fathers and sons. In short, it is Egyptians who torture Egyptians, Arabs who abuse Arabs.

Unfortunately, reflections of this kind were wholly lost in the farcical slanging match that erupted between Egypt and Kuwait over the torture of the two Egyptians. "Egyptian writers fiercely attacked Kuwait as if they suddenly discovered that the 'Egyptian citizen has dignity,'" the Kuwaiti journalist Fouad Al-Hashem wrote in *Al-Watan,* pointing to Egypt's own miserable record. The Egyptian writer Nasrat Sadek promptly shot back in the independent *Al-Masry Al-Youm,* titling his piece: "Egyptians Taught Them and They Paid Them Back in Torture." As it happens, he did not mean "taught them torture"—he merely meant to say that the 400,000 or so Egyptian expatriate workers who live in tiny Kuwait "participated in its development." The editor in chief of *El-Esboa* and member of the Egyptian parliament, Mustafa Bakri, actually tabled a question in parliament to Foreign Minister Ahmed Aboul Gheit about Al-Hashem's column, saying that the Kuwaiti writer "abused press freedom" by "insulting Egypt and its citizens." But that very same month, Cairo's governor shut down the Association for Human Rights Legal Aid, a group that looked after torture victims, after dubious allegations of financial irregularities. There it is in a nutshell: The messengers are being shot left, right, and center, while the regime redoubles its abuses with demented vigor.

CHAPTER SIX

CORRUPTION

A certain degree of respect, of a perverse type, must be given the Egyptian government as it watches diligently to unearth any potential threat that would tarnish the good name of Egypt and the Egyptians. Such was the case in 2007 when an organization called the New Seven Wonders Foundation announced the final round of online voting for a list of what it had been billing for a full five years as the New Seven Wonders of the World. What offended the Egyptian government? What made it go ballistic? The Giza Pyramids would not be included automatically as part of the New Seven Wonders, and instead would be listed as just one of the various candidates.

Following the barrage of complaints by the Egyptian Culture Ministry, backed by a concerted (if ultimately, as ever, contrived) campaign of vilification on the part of the government-controlled press, the poll's creator, one Bernard Weber, appeared to backtrack. "After careful consideration, the New Seven Wonders Foundation designates the Pyramids of Giza—the only original wonder of the world remaining—an honorary New Seven

Wonder," he explained in a letter *Al-Ahram* said he sent to Culture Minister Farouk Hosni. As a sign of respect, the decision, he reportedly added, took into consideration the views of Egypt's Supreme Council of Antiquities and the Culture Ministry, both of which had insisted that, since the pyramids are "a shared world culture and heritage site," they warrant "special status."

Hosni was elated at the U-turn, and could not resist having a final stab at the New Seven Wonders Foundation. It had launched its campaign, he apparently claimed, solely to make money from voters logging on to its Web site. "We must protect our heritage from amateurs and abusers who are always trying to take advantage of it," he declared.

However shrill and overblown, the Culture Ministry's response, looked at in a certain way, was understandable. As the only surviving Wonder, the pyramids are indeed unique; and the prospect, however remote, of their status as such being undermined by a bunch of ignoramuses voting on a Web site must have seemed to the Egyptian authorities an affront. On another, more significant level, though, the response smacked of hypocrisy. After all, with the tourism industry one of the Egyptian economy's main money earners, the Egyptian government itself puts the pyramids, along with the Egyptian Museum and the Nile, center stage in its own worldwide tourism marketing strategy geared toward nothing if not boosting the treasury's coffers. Moreover, in an age in which branding can go a long way to shaping perceptions of a country by outsiders, the endless tourism campaigns, coupled with Egyptian-sponsored television documentaries about the pharaonic past, subliminally help hoodwink the world into perceiving Egypt as a passive land of smiles, hospitality, sunshine, and ancient monuments, rather than the despotic, repressive, poverty-ridden mess on the brink of a popular uprising and ruled over by a brutal regime that it is in reality. The bid to maintain such false appearances, to promote the iconic image over complex reality, similarly lies behind the endless criminal trials of Egyptian journalists, reformers, and human rights workers who dare to criticize Mubarak, his family, or the military establishment, usually under the law that, with awful oppressive vagueness, prohibits any activity or even speech deemed by the regime as having "tarnished Egypt's image abroad."

The apparent hypocrisy of Hosni's reaction, however, goes deeper still. As anyone who has actually visited the pyramids can testify, corruption and general incompetence has left the last remaining of the Seven Wonders firmly in the grip of amateurs and abusers desperately trying to take advantage of Egypt's heritage. For a start, Egyptologists have long complained that the pyramids have suffered more damage in Egypt's brief period of mass tourism than in all the preceding four thousand years. However, amateurs begin the exploitation of tourists wanting see what is left of the pyramids a kilometer or so before they arrive at the site: Touts dive onto the side of taxis in a bid to persuade their occupants to take a tour after telling them that the official ticketing office is closed or some similar cock-and-bull story. The hassle increases once the tourists are inside the main gate, where more touts follow them about with the persistence of flies swarming around rotting trash. The security force on guard, whose job officially is to protect tourists from such unwanted attention, casually look the other way, unless a tourist finally loses his cool and causes a scene, in which case a cop will bark a mild admonishment at the tout. They have made a deal with the touts to pocket a percentage of whatever money is made from those tourists who do give in to their demands and finally, usually out of exasperation, opt to take a horse ride or have a photograph taken.

All this may seem trivial. But in 1997 such corruption at the bottom end of the tourism industry helped to allow a band of heavily armed jihadists to breeze their way through numerous police and army checkpoints leading to the Hatshepsut Temple, near Luxor. There they proceeded to massacre dozens of tourists and Egyptians before escaping into the desert unhindered. Before the attack, the priority of many local soldiers and cops had been to extract bribes from locals working with tour groups, smoke cigarettes, and sleep away the long hot summer afternoons in the backs of their vans. After the attack, it was again the image of the country, rather than the well-being of those who had been caught up in the violence, that seemed to take precedence. Knowing that a picture speaks a thousand words, the government forces, according to eyewitnesses widely quoted at the time, put most of their effort into finding and confiscating camcorders and cameras from everyone in the vicinity, lest an image of one of the acts of butchery carried out by the terrorists—they shot the tourists and then hacked them to pieces—found its way to a Western media outlet, and thus perhaps tarnish Egypt's carefully cultivated image abroad once and for all. Hundreds of tourists had been at the site during the attack. Almost all of them presumably had cameras. But not a single image of the atrocity has since become available, even on the Web.

However, it is when foreign tourists, many of whom are on their first trip to the Arab world, make it to the Egyptian Museum that they unwittingly enter the black heart of a regime in which amateurs and abusers make it their very lucrative business to take crude advantage of Egypt's unique heritage. Traditionally a classic example of Egyptian disorganization on a grand scale, the museum in downtown Cairo has provided the setting for a pillaging of the country's heritage on an almost unimaginable scale.

The Egyptian Museum's basement is a cavernous warren of rooms and corridors the size of a large cemetery that contains some sixty-five thousand antiquities, including one thousand coffins, some of them in boxes that have not been opened for seventy years. Most of the antiquities are believed to date from the most important dynasties of ancient Egypt; some of them have been exhibited before but had to be moved to make room upstairs for other artifacts; still others have never been seen in public. There they sit under inches of dust, cramped and often badly damaged by decades of neglect and poor ventilation and to all intents and purposes forsaken, if not quite forgotten.

Until the Supreme Council of Antiquities established new store rooms for newly discovered antiquities in all Egyptian governorates, this was where everything that was found under the sand went. The man who now rules over these treasures is Dr. Zahi Hawass, an Emmy laureate. His mighty nose and Indiana Jones hat are a constant presence on television screens and newspaper pages. Using his considerable exposure, Hawass has undertaken a personal and highly commendable battle against the corruption in his midst, while making headline-grabbing demands for the return of Egyptian antiquities held in museums abroad as well as for an inventory of the treasures it already has in hand. However, when some thirty-eight pieces reportedly went missing from the cellars of the museum itself in 2004, officials denied any such thing could happen. Hawass himself said making an inventory would take at least five months, while the process of overhauling the basement would take a year, by which time the missing thirty-eight pieces, he hoped, would probably turn up. Those in charge of developing the basement promptly found, though, that 70 percent of the antiquities decaying there had never been registered at all.

In such circumstances, it is frighteningly easy for pieces to disappear. Indeed, one worker was reportedly caught trying to sell three priceless pieces that he had hidden in bags of dust he was carrying out of the building in a minor clean-up operation. Some officials blamed a decrease in the

number of caretakers, each of whom is now responsible for overseeing between ten- and forty-thousand antiquities. According to Hawass, no inventory had been made of the Egyptian Museum for fifty years or more,
because everyone was afraid of being held to account if the stores proved
incomplete or the antiquities were found to be unregistered. In fact, until
1983 Egyptian antiquities were officially sold at auction and passed openly
through airports; and this is unlikely to have stopped altogether after the
country officially outlawed their export. Although there was an ambitious
project adopted in 1994 by one of Hawass's predecessors, Abdul-Halim
Nour Al-Deen, to inventory all sites, stores, and museums, backed by a
ministerial decree, the project ground to a halt once he left office. Al-Deen
said an inventory had been made of many of the antiquities, and that he
laid down a plan for making inventories of small museums and sites once
every year and of big museums once every four years. In fact, Hawass believes, only 10 to 15 percent of Egyptian antiquities were ever subjected to
an inventory, meaning that up to 85 percent were not, and could therefore
possibly disappear at any moment without a trace.

Enter Tarek Mohammed (a.k.a. Tarek Al-Sweisy). Deep mystery shrouds
Al-Sweisy's rise from a humble worker in an antiques bazaar on Cairo's Al-
Gomhouriya Street to an estimated wealth of more than $50 million, a
thirty-acre palace in the Abou Rawash area of Al-Haram (the district
around the pyramids), and the position of National Democratic Party secretary in that constituency. In his palace, authorities were to find not only
the pharaonic antiquities with which he had decorated it but also priceless
paintings from the Islamic eras (not to mention a cache of unlicensed
weapons). What is certain is that Al-Sweisy did not act alone: There were

no fewer than thirty-one codefendants in the case eventually brought against him, including antiquities inspectors and police officers. Of course, it was not Egyptian authorities who uncovered the smuggling operations, but police in Switzerland, who had suspected there was something odd about the contours of a piece of cargo that arrived in a Swiss airport with no data and no recipient specified on the packaging. The Swiss investigation found that Al-Sweisy had smuggled altogether two hundred and eighty rare antiquities in parcels through Cairo's Customs and Goods Village, with the help of an ordinary export company.

Talk about tarnishing the reputation of Egypt: Caught by foreigners smuggling the national patrimony, antiquities, was a prominent businessman and member of the ruling political party to boot. This clearly stood as an indictment of the regime, but indicting such a prominent man was not something to take lightly. The forces of Egyptian law and order ground into gear. A delegation from the Supreme State Security, the prosecution, and Interpol, which included several antiquities experts, set off to Switzerland to investigate. It found that the loot consisted of artifacts of great historic importance, including the contents of an entire tomb. In addition, there was the upper half of a statue representing Betah, remnants of the head of the goddess Sekhmet, a rare statue of goddess of love Aphrodite, two statues of colored wood representing the god Horus in the shape of a falcon, and even two intact mummies, all dating back to various ancient periods—pharaonic, Greek, and Roman—and officially falling under the useless protection of Egyptian law. All had been excavated stealthily at major archaeological sites and were without a registration number from the Supreme Antiquities Council. Many of them had been roughly handled. While some, especially the mummies, were in danger of decaying, most of them were still in good condition, since they came from dry desert areas, and could probably be saved.

According to a major report published by Kifaya in 2005 on corruption in Egypt, the Supreme State Security Prosecution's report ran to some three thousand five hundred pages, including the confessions of suspects arrested in the case, and contained, besides the smuggling charges, allegations of money laundering and possession of drugs and weapons.

Cairo's Criminal Court in the end sentenced Al-Sweisy to thirty-five years in jail and fined him three quarters of a million dollars for theft, smuggling, and hiding of antiquities, bribery, using forged documents, and money laundering. A Luxor public relations manager got fifteen years and a $9,000 fine. And Mohammed Sayyid Hassan got twenty years and a $9,000 fine. These sentences were reduced on appeal.

***

In certain ways, such corruption is amusing. The sheer inventiveness of some of the offenders, the shamelessness, the assumption that nobody actually dies from it however wrong it may be: All this can make it seem like a sort of nudge-wink experience anybody would secretly enjoy if they were lucky enough to get the opportunity. In the right circumstances, indeed, one might even take advantage of it oneself, given how unpleasant it can be when everybody insists on the rules all the time. For it offers a convenient way around the paperwork for petty infractions, a shortcut through often unreasonable and certainly antiquated regulations; and it can therefore be difficult even for people who try to be ethical to tell where it starts to get serious. What is for sure is that in the Arab world without *wasta*—"connections"—it is almost impossible to get anything done: Who you know, not what you know, is the name of the game. Instead of spending weeks waiting for things to get processed from desk to empty desk in the Byzantine bureaucracies, why not ring a cousin's brother-in-law in the ministry to get things expedited?

I got to taste the addictive convenience of *wasta* when, in 2006, I became acquainted for about six months in Cairo with the brother of a high-ranking general in the Egyptian army, who took me under his wing. Instead of spending a day or more at the Kafkaesque Mugamma government building in Tahrir Square renewing my visa, being shuttled from window to window and floor to floor by staff who took pride in their obstinacy and rudeness, the brother would call beforehand and I would be met at the entrance by a minion, who would then whisk me up directly to the office of the general in charge that day. There I would sit, sipping tea and munching on a biscuit, while my passport was given VIP-style fast-track treatment, and then returned fifteen minutes later—not with the six-month extension I had requested, but a year-long residence visa and, on the facing page, a multiple entry–reentry stamp. On my way to a moulid, or saint's festival, in Upper Egypt, an army conscript at a checkpoint had insisted that I wait a few hours for a military convoy to become available that would ride with me and my driver the last five kilometers, according to some rule he could not explain; but a quick phone call to the general's brother sent him scurrying to his boss, who promptly appeared in person, saluted me, told me to give his best wishes to my friend General So-and-So, and bid me on my immediate way in the company of one of his own armed guards. Most extraordinarily, when I lost my wallet in a microbus (a kind of minivan that serves as public transport) in Luxor and, having to get an official police report for insurance purposes but finding the tourism police on duty far from cooperative, I called the brother of General So-and-So, and his scolding of the officer on charge not only resulted in the immediate improvement of the treatment I received but also, a day later and to my utter astonishment, to the recovery of the wallet itself, which was handed over to me personally by the head of the tourism police, who had apparently made his way to the office for that task alone. Such reactions on the part of officials are not solely the result of fear: They know that by complying with such requests they will be able to pull in a favor at a later date from the general they were assisting. In Egypt, just as who you know matters more than what you know, what goes around surely comes around, too.

Yet it takes only a baby step for people to die, or at least fall seriously ill, as a result of corruption. A case in point occurred in 2006. Fayiz Hamad was a pupil in Makram Al-Akhlaq primary school until he was hospitalized in Marsa Matrouh public hospital after he was given a compulsory dose of vaccines by a group of people apparently prowling the streets in an unidentified car and claiming they had to find children who qualified for the treatment, which was part of an immunization campaign (according to a complaint filed by his father). Dr. Abbas Al-Shanawani, a Health Ministry undersecretary, promptly announced that the child had been put under twenty-four-hour care, his stomach was immediately pumped, and samples were taken from his blood and vomit and sent for analysis to central labs in the ministry as a precautionary measure. The ministry insisted there had been no program of compulsory vaccination anywhere during that period and any rumors to the contrary were completely groundless and merely aimed at spreading panic among the populace. *Al-Wafd* newspaper disagreed, citing ample testimony from people that there had been compulsory vaccinations carried out at the time, and not just in the village but in Cairo as well. They said the officials would simply go around the houses and inject children, who would later come down with a high temperature, vomiting, and diarrhea, with some of them having to be hospital-ized. *Al-Arabi Al-Nasseri* newspaper claimed that the reason was that the drugs were spoiled.

According to the Kifaya report, the Central Auditing Bureau found that one vaccination company had imported some $4 million worth of ex-pired vaccines, while some 370,000 bottles of the vaccine valued at roughly $500,000 were sitting in the company's stores without a production or ex-piration date on the packaging. Plasma and blood derivatives were stored for three years although the shelf life was no more than one year, and were imported from the United Kingdom although Egypt bans such imports from there. If true these are obviously serious accusations with very seri-ous consequences.

The only tangible outcome of the scandal was that Hatem Al-Gabaly, the minister of Housing and Health, promised a project for proper storage of drugs with the participation of a pharmacists' syndicate to end random distribution and protect citizens from fake, expired, and smuggled drugs.

Egyptian journalists working for independent and opposition newspapers have done some of their best work in recent years unearthing stories of cor-ruption, including that which permeates the main state-run dailies, where employment strategies traditionally often have had little do with merit and a great deal to do with *wasta:* the accusation is that big *wasta* apparently gets you a position on *Al-Ahram,* the main daily; less-but-still-considerable *wasta* can get you a position on *Al-Akhbar;* lowly contacts means you have to settle for the trashy *Al-Gomhouriya.* Such a culture of nepotism goes some way to explaining the decline in the quality of the state-owned news-papers; and the space they leave for unearthing corruption likewise explains much of the growth of the opposition media. However, in 2005 the state-controlled media was forced to air its own dirty laundry. The Prosecutor General's Office and the Public Funds Investigating Attorney launched probes into corruption at the Media Production City, and parliament's anticorruption task force started investigating corruption allegations at the three leading state-owned daily news organizations. The allegations had come to light in opposition newspapers after a government-ordered shake-up sent their long-serving editors in chief into retirement. There was some suspicion surrounding the timing of the allegations and indeed it is possible all the allegations were politically expedient. Was the regime itself behind the leaks in a bid to destroy the credibility of editors who as insiders had been controllable but who were now potential threats out in the wilderness?

It comes as a surprise that a veteran columnist at *Al-Ahram*, Salama Ahmed Salama, is perhaps the only Egyptian journalist who commands the respect of his colleagues right across the political spectrum, to the extent that he is often interviewed on local political developments in the opposition media. When I met him in his office in the *Al-Ahram* building in late 2006 to discuss corruption and nepotism in the state-run media, I first asked him how he had managed to survive all these years despite highlighting the issue of corruption and criticizing the regime in many other areas as well. "I think they are intelligent enough to leave a certain margin for some individuals to take a critical attitude toward the policies of the regime," Salama told me.

> It's a kind of manipulation of the situation, in order always to give the impression that there is freedom of expression and freedom of opinion. This way, whenever they take any measures against the editors of opposition newspapers, for example, they can say that they are doing so only be-

cause they went beyond what is permitted by the law. Of course, the justice system here can in a way also be manipulated by the government, and they can drag the trial on for years and years. But as long as I'm not taking an overtly hostile attitude to the government, as long as I am not a Muslim Brother or a Communist or have another radical agenda, they leave me to offer rational criticism, for example in favor of us going farther down the road to democracy. That's something they claim they are in favor of anyway, so I use their own terminology in order to show that what they are doing is not what they are claiming to do. I think this strategy gives me a lot of maneuverability.

What is it like writing for a newspaper where the editor in chief is appointed by the president, and usually ends up being more royal than the royals?

He laughed:

The editors in chief are very cautious, to the point of being cowards. They don't even use the margins of freedom that they've been given. Whatever they write, nobody believes them. And what they write is usually very weak anyway. They are in constant fear that they might be thrown out of their job and so would lose all the privileges that come with it—the financial privileges, the prestige, being invited by the president to go with him on his private plane, attending meetings with foreign heads of state (although they never ask a proper question at the press conferences at such meetings because they are mediocre).

I reminded him of the big scandal involving his former boss, the editor in chief of *Al-Ahram,* Ibrahim Nafia, and his infamous $500,000 monthly salary, and wanted to know if corruption on the newspaper is really as bad as that example would suggest. Salama confirmed that indeed it is. "The first problem is that all of these state-owned newspapers depend very heavily on advertising to make money," he sighed.

> For example, there are many adverts for luxury housing in *Al-Ahram*. I wrote a column about how the whole building industry is geared around the superrich. They go around the country building very luxurious villas and apartment blocks only for those who are millionaires. I said that this destroys the fabric of our society. Where can a young person buy an apartment in order to get married? Where will he find the half million pounds? The next day I was introduced to this guy who is a big shot in the National Democratic Party and a millionaire or billionaire or whatever. He tried to convince me that what I wrote was wrong by saying that while they build for rich people they also build for those on other levels of society. I told him that I'm not going to retract what I wrote because my argument was substantiated by facts and figures, which show that the smallest apartment being built these days costs something like a quarter of a million pounds, and even that's way outside of the city in the middle of the desert. And this, you see, is precisely how the corruption then feeds in. It was made clear that it would be very easy, if I agreed to write a retraction, for the man then to arrange for me to get an apartment, but I would have to shut my mouth from then on.

He would actually have given you an apartment?

Oh, yes! This kind of thing is happening here in *Al-Ahram* all the time. It's very difficult to keep your hands clean. There are journalists in this building who have done just that. I know it for a fact. They get apartments. Not exactly as gifts, of course. But take that apartment for half a million: The journalist will 'buy' it for one hundred thousand, then sell it for the market price and make a huge profit. The construction companies even do this with ministers, so why not with journalists? One Western-style compound has been sold exclusively to ministers at a knockdown price. Remember that many journalists have very low salaries. They have to find some way of boosting their income.

If some journalists on the government-owned newspapers are corrupt, it stands to reason, I pointed out, that they will have no motive in exposing the same kind of corruption in the government.

This is obviously true. But there has been one positive outcome. The situation has given a big opportunity to the opposition newspapers. They excel in this area by filling the gap in the coverage. But it's for this reason that they don't get advertising revenues, and they don't get access to government officials. This in turn creates another vicious cycle: Because the government gives them the runaround and treats them like naughty children, journalists on the opposition newspapers working on corruption stories can't get quotes from the officials and so have to go with whatever information they've got. Then when the articles appear, the government turns around and says they've got the facts wrong and sends them to court.

The Fund for Peace (FfP), a Washington-based independent educational, research, and advocacy organization, ranked Egypt thirty-sixth out of one hundred and seventy-seven states in a failed states index published in July 2007. State failure can either mean the government has lost physical control over the country's territory, as in Somalia and Afghanistan, or it has lost the authority to execute decisions, provide the public with services, and act as a cohesive entity and the only single representative of a people in the international arena. The FfP uses twelve indicators to measure state failure, and Egypt scored a stellar nine out of ten in criminalization or delegitimization of the state, understood as "massive and endemic corruption or profiteering by ruling elites, resistance of ruling elites to transparency, accountability and political representation, widespread loss of popular confidence in state institutions, and processes and growth of crime syndicates linked to ruling elites." It rated 8.5 out of ten in "suspension or arbitrary application of the rule of law and widespread violation of human rights." And it rated a relatively modest 8.3 in the "rise of factionalized elites" or the "fragmentation of elites and state institutions along group lines," and the use of "nationalistic political rhetoric by ruling elites."

"Corruption in Egypt is widespread, ranging from taxi drivers trying to make an extra buck to [parliamentarians] accusing the ruling National Democratic Party of rigging the 2005 elections, in which Hosni Mubarak, president since 1981, 'won' a fourth term by having himself re-nominated by parliament, then confirmed without opposition in a referendum," the FfP's Egypt country profile says. Magdy Al-Galad, the editor in chief of the independent daily *Al-Masry Al-Youm,* told a seminar titled "Towards Enhancing Transparency in Local Markets" that was held at the same time of the report's publication: "There is a corruption-related case reported every two minutes in Egypt, and only ten percent of those types of violations get caught." Salah Diab, the newspaper's owner, was quoted as telling the same seminar: "There is a type of corruption that causes little damage in society, like paying five pounds to an officer to avoid a ticket, and then there is the harmful corruption, the type that leads to lost opportunities." But in Egypt, there exists in fact no such distinction. "Corruption is the result of a corrupting process, and ignoring this is like trying to cure a disease without tackling its root cause," added combative Egyptian journalist Amin Howeidy in *Al-Ahram Weekly.* "A strong state will . . . safeguard the security of its citizens, not only its rulers. And it will, with equal efficacy, counter internal and external threats while inducing both governing and governed to respect its laws, money and possessions." Such a state, according to Howeidy, will resist both corruption and those seeking to corrupt. In so doing, "it removes the impediments to progress, given that corruption will impede all economic development and healthy investment." Howeidy cites the example of law number 175 for the year 2005. "This stipulates that a member of parliament cannot be employed in a government or public sector position, nor can he work in a foreign company while he is an MP. Article 158 of this law asserts that 'a minister cannot buy or lease anything using the financial resources of the state.' Such are the safeguards against the abuse of power, but are they upheld?"

That they are not is the thrust of a massive report by the reform group *Kifaya* published in 2006, which motivated various other organizations to focus on corruption. If the two-hundred-page report, from which the examples above about the stolen artifacts and drugs scandals are taken, is, as Middle East expert Barry Rubin has pointed out, a largely unreadable rag-bag of reflection, upside-down documentation, sometimes self-contradictory inference and lament—at one point it actually launches into verse—it is partly because Kifaya is a small disparate organization of Cairo intellectuals run on a shoestring and beset with constant problems and harassment; but it is mostly because corruption in Egypt is giant, amorphous, and finally ungraspable.

The report covers corruption in finance, business, culture, and the media. It sets out what it says was the distribution of carcinogenic insecticides by the Ministry of Agriculture between 1981 and 2003; lists the fugitive businessmen and MPs said to be involved in unsecured loan schemes worth billions of dollars; dissects the allegedly corruption-riddled sale of the American-Egyptian Bank; documents what it says is the blatant manipulation of inflation and unemployment figures over twenty-five years of mismanagement of the economy; pinpoints widespread negligence and incompetence of underpaid doctors in the public health system; and veers on occasion into torture and the plight of street children, of which there are a million in Cairo alone. Like torture and the abuse of power, to which it is so closely linked, corruption is a disease that has long spread to all of Egypt's organs. There is literally no end to it; it reaches precisely from the officer who takes five pounds to overlook a speeding offense all the way to the top, swelling in magnitude as it infests the ranks and stopping arguably only with Mubarak, the most corrupt offender of them all, because there is no one above him— "arguably" because, cynics might say, his paymasters in the United States are ultimately even more corrupt in propping up his regime while making a great to-do about promoting democracy in places whose current leadership is less conducive to its Middle East agenda. What emerges from the Kifaya report, and becomes clear to anyone who spends time in Egypt, is that the infection has spread to vast numbers of its people, and certainly those in official positions, who are exactly as bent as their position will allow and would gladly be a lot more corrupt if they had any more influence to peddle.

"There is a tide in the affairs of men," says Brutus, "which, taken at the flood, leads on to fortune." It was perhaps mindful of this Shakespearean dictum that the World Bank and the International Finance Corporation in late 2007 awarded Egypt the coveted title of "world's top reformer" in the report *Doing Business 2008*. Compiled, it would seem, during the brief, tenure of that hero of democracy and one of the alleged architects of the

Iraq war, Paul Wolfowitz, as World Bank president, the assessment hailed the Egyptian government for having "pulled out all the stops. . . . Its efforts cut deep." Egypt topped the table by making more economic reforms in the 2006–2007 period than any other country surveyed. The report looked at ten different areas of business regulation in one hundred and seventy-eight countries, tracking the time and cost needed to meet government requirements in business start-up, operation, trade, taxation, and closure. Egypt was considered to have made significant progress in five areas: improving the process of starting a business, licensing, property registration, obtaining credit, trading across borders, and business closure. Several reforms made it easier to start a business in Egypt, including a huge cut in the minimum capital required to do so from $8,930 to $180. The average start-up time and costs were halved to nine days and $385. For the compilers of the report, particularly praiseworthy legislative changes included the reduction of red tape in getting building licenses and the establishment of one-stop service centers for exporters and importers and other businessmen and investors at the country's ports. The cost of registering property has also been cut, leading to a 39 percent increase in registration fee income for the authorities in the first six months after the reform was introduced. A new private credit bureau has also been established, which is to improve credit access, particularly for small- and medium-sized enterprises and micro companies.

While some niggled that Egypt reformed quickly over the past year because it started from a low base of significant overregulation—since, in other words, from 0.0 to 0.1 is in fact an infinite leap impossible to match by a mere improvement from middling to fair—Michael Klein, World Bank–IFC vice president for financial and private sector development, said categorically: "Investors are looking for upside potential and they find it in economies that are reforming, regardless of their starting point." So much for Howeidy's naïve conviction that "corruption will impede all economic development and healthy investment." Of course, it is difficult to fault the World Bank for alerting its majority shareholders in the West when there is a yard sale on. Klein duly noted that "equity returns are highest in the countries that are reforming the fastest"—not least, it should be added, the massive artificial gains for stock speculators in the days after the study was released.

Even so, it is difficult for some to see why Egypt should be given quite such an attention-grabbing high ranking (ahead of China and Bulgaria) since anyone but the swiftest hit-and-run corporate raiders would find themselves in deep trouble if they actually went ahead and followed it. "Even by Middle Eastern standards, Egypt has never been an easy place to do business" read a more sober assessment that appeared two years earlier in *Newsweek,* a publication rarely accused of rabid antimarket bias. "Its inwardly focused economy has stagnated for the past seven years. Inflation is rife, tariffs and unemployment are among the highest in the world, and red tape is endless." While absurdly pinning its hopes at the time on Gamal Mubarak, it nevertheless offered a rather more realistic view of the business situation, saying the result of the reforms then already under way was at best "a new sense of hope about Egypt's prospects and its effect on the region." It added a crucial caveat: "Of course, it's easy to be overly optimistic when it comes to Egyptian reform. The country has a history of false promises and backtracking dating to the 1970s." Investment Minister Mahmoud Mohieldin, *Newsweek* reported, announced an ambitious privatization program for the following year, including at least one state-owned bank and possibly Telecom Egypt. "But even if he can stick to his timeline," it added, "experts are doubtful about economic change without further political reform."

Yet two years later, the World Bank, in the obligatory "needs improvement" bit of their report, could only bring itself to lament that, while workers are relatively easy to hire, they remain somewhat difficult to fire by regional and global standards—"taking away any incentive to create jobs." "Any incentive": There can be no business school in the world, however dogmatic, that regards as the sole incentive for creating jobs the pleasure of taking them away again. *Doing Business 2008* also bemoans that a medium-sized company spends 711 hours in tax-payment procedures annually, compared to an average of 236.8 hours and 183.3 hours in the region and Organization for Economic Cooperation and Development member states respectively. And even for the asset strippers, Egypt lags sorely behind in the ease and cost of business closure, the average period being 4.2 years, compared to 3.7 years in the region as a whole and 1.3 years in OECD member states. Average costs are high in Egypt, at 20.0 percent of GNI per capita, compared to 13.9 percent in the region and 7.5 percent in OECD member countries—but bear in mind that per capita GNI is tiny compared to them. To compound this, however, recovery rates on closed businesses were very low, at 16.6 cents on the dollar, as opposed to 25.8 cents and 74.1 cents in the respective comparable groups.

There are a number of possible explanations for the contents and tone of the World Bank report. One, no doubt too paranoid to contemplate seriously, is that the former World Bank president, or those he serves, saw in its publication an opportunity to reward Egypt for its assistance in the "war on terror" at the time when he was still U.S. deputy secretary of defense. Another is that the World Bank, far from being a beacon of international financial probity, is in fact a fringe cult of free-market extremists who hold that transparency and accountability are marginal to good business: a kind of Branch Davidians of international finance, with all the self-contradictions and sheer walleyed stupidity that entails and the report displays. Whatever the truth of the matter, *Doing Business 2008* provides a textbook example of how the Mubarak regime is able to blithely continue its abuse of every principle ever signed up to by the international community. Of course, the reforms look good on paper; any superficial observer might be taken in. The problem with corruption is that once it has become endemic it no longer matters one whit what the regulations say, and the frantic cutting of red tape merely increases the opportunities for the thieves who run the country to steal what little is still left to steal.

The last word on the matter of corruption in Egypt should not go to the international bankers but to an Egyptian novelist, Sonalla Ibrahim, who summed up the issue and the role of individual accountability within it in front of the culture minister and leading Arab intellectuals when he was awarded the prize of the 2003 Novel Conference:

> We have no theatre, cinema, scientific research or education. We have festivals, conferences, and a box of lies. We have no industry, agriculture, health, education, or justice; corruption and looting spread, and those who object are humiliated, beaten, and tortured. The exploitative minority among us plunged us into this horrible reality; amid this, the writer cannot shut his eyes and remain silent; he cannot abandon his responsibility. I won't ask you to issue a statement that condemns and protests, because those are no longer useful; I won't ask you to do anything, because you know better than me what should be done. All I can do is to thank again the great professors who have honored me by choosing me for the prize, and declare that I am sorry I cannot accept it, because it is issued by a government that I think does not have the credibility to issue it.

CHAPTER SEVEN

LOST DIGNITY

E gypt's most celebrated living movie director, Youssef Chahine, was born in 1926, brought up in a middle-class Christian household in the cosmopolitan city of Alexandria and educated at the prestigious Victoria College. On his return from studying cinema in Los Angeles he plunged into the local movie industry, then enjoying a boom during the last years of King Farouk's reign. This eclectic director's liberal humanism can be traced back to the diversity and relative freedom of the prerevolutionary period into which he was fortunate to be born. But following the revolution, he became another genius working under a brutal authoritarianism that considers the creative instinct at best suspicious and at worst a threat that must be crushed. His more than forty movies, dating from before the 1952 coup, have helped define Egyptian identity, history, and memory. However, his refusal to suck up to the regime or bow to religious dogma, coupled with his frequent use of bisexual male and liberated female characters, has left him largely ostracized by the Egyptian movie industry and state-run mass media. Even before they had seen it, the Egyptian censors announced they would likely ban Chahine's latest movie, *Chaos* (2007), an angry, melodramatic story about the torture subculture in the country's police stations and the corruption with which it goes hand in hand. (The movie was eventually given a certificate for general release.) With *Chaos,* Chahine returned to the subject of his classic *The Sparrow* (1973), which blamed corruption for Egypt's defeat in the Six-Day War. That movie was banned on its release, although it was later awarded the country's highest cultural prize. In addition to facing regime hostility, Chahine has the unfortunate distinction of having uniquely had a movie banned in Egypt as a result of a protest orchestrated by both Muslim *and* Christian extremists: His biblical epic *The Emigrant* (1994), based on the life of the prophet Joseph, was attacked by Islamists using a 1983 fatwa issued by Al-Azhar outlawing representation of all prophets in any artistic work and by Copts claiming the portrayal of Joseph himself was "inaccurate."

That the eighty-two-year-old director now has nothing but contempt for the Egyptian military regime was evident in a rare, brief interview he gave with the German-based online magazine *Qantra* in 2006, in which he stated: "We live in a total dictatorship." He went on to lament that he has no hope that Egypt will become freer or more liberal in the future, and cast the country's young people as a mass of aimless souls who long only to leave the country. "I see them in front of the German and French consulates. Everybody wants to emigrate," he said. "I used to tell the young people: 'Don't do it! If you have studied, we need you here.' I was old-fashioned, thinking only of the beauty of my country. Now I tell them: 'Leave!' They have no chance here, it's too corrupt. By staying here, you become corrupt." That Chahine equates patriotism with an outdated mindset is perhaps the saddest, and most revealing, part of the interview.

Many in the West have also drawn attention to a mass obsession with emigration among so many different sections of Egypt's imploding society, to the millions who long to leave not only for France, Germany, and other European countries but also, indeed perhaps especially, for the country where Chahine learned his craft: America. This is proof, some have further argued, that Egyptians are not as anti-Western as often perceived by outsiders, which is to say not so angered by American policies in the region as is typically thought to be the case. But this kind of political point scoring largely misses the point. The real question is: Why do so many young Egyptians, *despite* their abstract hatred of the effects of U.S. regional hegemony and their personal anger at Washington for propping up their own dictator (all obvious to anyone who has spent any time in the country), still prefer to take their chances in the West? The obvious answer is that the hatred they hold for their own country is deeper than that which they hold for the foreign policies of the country they will be moving to: Culture and politics, personal ambition and political conviction, are not entwined as one in their minds. There is one thing, though, that all agree on, namely that, as Chahine clearly indicated, there is a massive urge to leave, especially although not exclusively among the young. In the 1990s, about two or three in every ten Egyptians I met spoke of their desire to live elsewhere. By 2007, virtually everyone I met was expressing a burning desire to emigrate, often within the first five minutes of our conversation.

One particular incident comes to mind: I hired a taxi driver in his twenties while in Aswan to take me on a trip to the High Dam, and we got on like old friends from the outset. On the way back to town, he suddenly pulled over, recited the whole of the opening verse of the Qur'an aloud with closed eyes, then turned to me and asked with painful seriousness: "Please can you get me a visa to travel to England?" After I gently explained that this was out of the question, not least because I myself have not been back to the country of my birth since leaving a decade earlier and had no plans to do so in the immediate future, he appeared to be genuinely devastated. In retrospect, it seems possible that the whole routine was just a charade performed for every Westerner with whom he struck up however brief a friendship; but that hardly undermines what is surely the extraordinary frustration behind his pleading. What he must have thought of my aversion to returning to the country he would have given a ransom to move to is anyone's guess. But even when I made it clear to a new acquaintance that I was not going to provide a bridge for him to escape to the West, the constant pestering continued. On my return to Egypt after a month-long trip to Iran, for instance, a guy in his twenties who came to my apartment to fix my computer suddenly asked me about the possibilities open for someone like him there. He had a degree in computer technology, he explained, was fluent in English, and had been trained by a major computer firm in software programming; but because he had no *wasta,* he was finding it impossible to get taken on by a major company. "Iran is even worse than Egypt," I told him. "The economy is going down the drain, and there's even less freedom there than there is here." He stared at the ground pensively for a few moments, then replied: "I don't care if I have to eat bread and water. I just want to live in a country where the people show me some respect when I walk in the street." The pestering for a visa from all and sundry became intensely annoying, and it was sometimes easy to lose sight of the sadness and despair that was their motivation.

An investigative report by the BBC in July 2007 found that thousands of young Egyptian men try to enter Europe illegally every year. Sometimes they set sail from the Egyptian coast aboard fishing boats run by people smugglers. Mostly, though, they undertake the perilous crossing to Italy from neighboring Libya, a country they do not need a visa to visit. Needless to say, poverty, unemployment, and a general sense of hopelessness and helplessness were the reasons the report gave for this willingness to risk their lives. In November 2007, the accuracy of the BBC investigation was confirmed when Egypt was plunged into national mourning at the news that at least twenty-two Egyptians trying to make their way to Italy illegally to find work drowned after their boat capsized.

When a legal opportunity to leave arises, Egyptians unsurprisingly make the most of it, and some are prone to employing illegal methods to extend their stay. (I never met a young man who did not freely admit that if he ever got the chance to leave there was no way he would return voluntarily.) The results have made for international headlines. In August 2006, for instance, the FBI and U.S. Immigration and Customs Enforcement alerted intelligence agencies and state and local law enforcement about eleven Egyptian students who had failed to report to their classes at Montana State University after they entered the country through New York's John F. Kennedy International Airport. They were scheduled to take English and American history courses as part of an exchange program with Mansoura University in Upper Egypt. The students had been required to register with the university under a Student and Exchange Visitor Program set up after the terror attacks of September 11, with the aim of ensuring that only legitimate foreign students are granted entry into the United States. Several of the hijackers on September 11 had listed their occupations as student on their visa forms. Eventually, the Egyptian students were located and arrested for violating the terms of their visas, as well as immigration regulations. They were swiftly deported. But terrorism, it turned out, had been the last thing on their minds: They had fled in pursuit, as *Al-Ahram Weekly* nicely put it, of "the American dream," dropping out of the immersion courses to try to find work and apparently intending to survive in the meantime on the $3,500 they had been given as part of the exchange deal for living expenses. The extensive and sometimes sensational publicity surrounding that case, in both the United States and Egypt, evidently did nothing to deter two Egyptian heavyweight boxers from similarly abandoning their teammates in October 2007 after they arrived in the United States to take part in the World Boxing Championships. Abdel-Halim and Ahmed Samir also went missing shortly after the team landed at a U.S. airport. But this time, no national alert was issued by the FBI. So many Egyptian athletes, mainly boxers and wrestlers, had previously gone AWOL in similar circumstances to seek a better environment in which to develop their skills that, on this occasion, the flight of the two boxers appears to have provoked little more than an acknowledgment from the U.S. authorities. The most striking thing about these individuals is that, unlike those who set sail from Libya, they are hardly the impoverished equivalents of, say, illegal immigrants from sub-Saharan Africa crammed into rickety boats bound for the Canary Islands, or Mexicans who spend days in the desert in an attempt to make their way across the porous U.S.-Mexican border. These students were studying at one of Egypt's most respected state-run universities; and they were held in such high regard by their academic supervisors that they were granted much sought-after scholarships. The boxers likewise had risen so high in their profession that they could compete in international competitions.

If individuals such as these are willing to risk losing everything they have achieved in their bid to escape from Egypt, to what lengths will the impoverished masses who have little to lose go, short of clambering into a fishing boat on the waters of the Mediterranean with only a hope and a prayer? The answer to that question, it turns out, is to be found in Luxor, Egypt's best known and historically most popular tourist resort. In recent years, the city has also been transformed into the male prostitution capital of the Middle East.

Luxor has long had a reputation as the Sin City of Egypt. Archaeologists from Johns Hopkins University, presently working in the local Temple of Mut, have shown how sex and booze were key aspects of rites carried out by the locals to appease the pharaonic-era gods. According to the archeologists, the rituals involved getting drunk on barley beer and then "traveling through the marshes" (a euphemism for having sex) before passing out and rousing themselves the next morning just in time for religious services. A more uncomfortable combination of booze, sex, and religion still largely defines life here—at least for the foreign visitors and the 90 percent of local males who work in the tourism industry, which completely dominates the local economy.

Luxor attracts mostly British and German sunseekers, who only occasionally leave their sundecks by the pool in their five-star hotels to mingle in the local souks with other foreign day-trippers whose cruise boats are moored along the broad and beautiful Nile. The Western package tourists are often mocked for not leaving their hotels by more adventurous travelers; and it is true that many of them could be anywhere for all they care, so long as there is winter sunshine and a disco to go to in the evening. Many do not even visit the local monuments. However, even the culturally curious among them, especially those with small children, usually opt not to venture out on their own a second time after their first encounter with the extraordinary hassle on the local streets. Nowhere else in the Arab world (perhaps the whole world) is it so aggressive and relentless.

Taxi drivers, touts, horse-and-carriage drivers, unemployed youths, pestering kids: they hang out on every street corner, waiting for any opportunity to come their way to make a few dollars so they can bring bread to the table. Tourism Minister Zoheir Garranah has been quoted as saying that hassle is a bigger threat to Egypt's tourism industry than the bombs of militants, and has acknowledged that many tourists, frustrated at being accosted by touts, leave the country "with a bitter taste and vowing never to return." Even for an Arabic speaker, peeling them off can prove a Herculean task, the last resort being a threat of violence.

For those who do get five minutes to themselves, though, the corniche along the Nile, stretching for kilometers and in pristine condition, is a wonderful place for a stroll, dotted as it is with landmarks such as the Winter Palace Hotel and the magisterial Luxor Temple. Those cruising down the Nile itself are afforded spectacular views of a city the river cuts in two. On the East Bank, or modern half of Luxor, are the main hotels, the airport, markets, and train station, all recently renovated with a substantial grant from UNESCO. On the impoverished West Bank, hidden in the Theban hills, are the legendary Valley of the Kings, Valley of the Queens, and Hatshepsut Temple, beyond which lie barren desert and mountains.

The populated areas of the West Bank, between the Nile and the tombs, are still largely fertile plains that roll back in lush green from the river: picture-postcard scenes of farmers working in sugarcane fields and little boys wearing *gelabiyas* and riding donkeys along the dirt tracks of mud-brick villages. To cross the Nile on the public ferry, from the East Bank to the West Bank, is to travel back in time: from the urban to the rural, the modern to the deeply traditional.

My friend Alaa—a small, rotund man in his late thirties with thick curly black hair—lived in one of the two villages closest to the Nile on the West Bank side of town. Everyone else in the enclave of his village was either a close or distant relative: This is tribal territory, and as in all of Upper Egypt the Muslims and Christians who live here are conservative and family-centered. In the mornings, Alaa worked as a teacher at the local government-run school. But I had gotten into the habit of sitting with him during the evenings on the other side of town, at the reception of a budget hotel where he also worked, and I had booked myself into it during one of my first trips to the city. A few months later, though, he had suddenly come to the realization that if he stayed at home in the evenings he would actually save money: His job at the hotel paid only $26 a month, an amount that failed to cover his transport to and from the East Bank and the two packets of cigarettes he would chain-smoke during his tedious twelve-hour shifts, not to mention the occasional sandwich.

As Alaa's circumstances and the street hassle indicate, the tourism industry in Egypt is a microcosm of the wider economy. A few dozen companies dominate the trade: from the buses that shuttle tour groups to and from the airport to the luxury hotels they stay in and the cruise boats they sail up and down the Nile on. Small fry like Alaa are left waiting for the crumbs that fall from the table. Alaa told me that he was very happy not to be pestering tourists anymore to take donkey rides, a hopeless side business he helped to run at the hotel. When he said this he smiled self-consciously, perhaps recollecting how he had spent the first half an hour with me describing the wonders (and cost) of such a trip around the West Bank at sunrise. He had also felt unhappy, he added, working at an establishment that sold beer in the bar upstairs. But now he could get a good night's sleep and spend quality time with his wife and new baby girl.

We sat on the roof of his half-built house and chatted away the evening, the sun slowly setting on the horizon. After a while, I mentioned the fact that almost all the buildings, both here and in the other village nearest the Nile, had been built recently, and a not inconsiderable number of them were luxury villas—strikingly different to the mud brick dwellings most farmers still lived in elsewhere on the West Bank. I was curious to learn where the owners had acquired their wealth.

"Ninety percent of all these houses and the land they're built on are owned by foreigners," Alaa told me. "All the young men here are now marrying older Western women."

On the East Bank, where I spent almost all of my time, I was used to seeing older Western women (usually in their fifties or sixties) walking hand in hand with local young studs, typically in their late teens or early twenties. I had assumed they were enjoying "holiday romances." But it appeared from what Alaa was saying that many actually lived here on the West Bank. Later I checked out the official figures: According to the Ministry of Justice, some thirty-five thousand Egyptians have indeed married foreigners, nearly three quarters being cross-cultural marriages involving Egyptian men and foreign women. That figure probably does not include *orfi,* or temporary, marriages, which are shunned as a form of legalized prostitution by Egyptians, but provide legal cover for the overwhelming majority of relationships between Egyptian men and foreign women. It means they can live together in an apartment, for example, without having to worry about the police banging on the door and thus ruining the reputation of their family by being accused of having sex out of wedlock. It also offers an implicit reassurance to the Egyptian women the men usually also marry, in addition to the Western women, that theirs is the "real" thing, as opposed to the marriages to foreigners, which are undertaken only for financial gain.

"But if they're married, there's no difference really," I told Alaa that evening. "They've got to marry someone, and if the woman has money, then all for the good."

"It makes a big difference," he retorted. "I see my village changing for the worse every day. Some of these women slept with half the men in Luxor before they settled on marrying one. Anyway, they are old enough to be their grandmothers! This never used to happen here. When I was young, the tourists who came here were respectful. You were honored to invite them to your home. These days, if you take any foreign females back to your village, even if they are good people, everyone thinks you are going to screw them."

But all that, he was eager to point out, was the least of his concerns.

"What I want to know is what's going to happen when their children grow up? We are traditional people. We have very strict rules here for our girls. They don't go out alone after dark. They don't have sex before marriage. Westerners don't have the same rules. Maybe the girls will grow up like some of their mothers, screwing every man who winks at them. We're losing our culture and our religion and nobody cares, as long as there's money to be made."

I thought about saying something about cultural integration and globalization, of the vibrant clash of the new and the old, and of posing the question of whether he thought poverty was a more viable option for these young men since there seemed to be no third option. Before I got chance to speak, though, Alaa had started up again.

"You know what is really on my mind?" he asked.

It's the question of the land. That bothers me even more than the culture. Almost all the land is being bought by the foreign women. The price is going up and up. Land prices here have doubled in the last five years. When my children grow up, how are they going to afford to buy land to build their own houses? We're going to be driven out in the end. It will be an exclusion zone: If you're not married to a foreigner, they won't even let you in for security reasons. Egyptians banned from their own land! And you know what that reminds me of? The Jews in Palestine. Read the history. Before 1948, the Jews acquired almost all the land they owned legally. Those Palestinians were the same as these Egyptians here in Luxor. And look what happened. In the end, the Palestinians were robbed of their land completely. We're being colonized through the back door.

One is reminded of the comment by Dr. Okasha, the Cairo psychiatrist: "Since ancient times, the Egyptian has been known as a man who never leaves his place. His honor is his land." If he loses his honor when he leaves his land, what does he lose when he sells it to an outsider, in addition to selling his body to an older foreign woman? The Tourism Ministry actually has a goal of selling ten thousand residential units a year to foreigners, a statistic that would no doubt send further shivers down Alaa's spine; but even the cross-cultural marriage phenomenon is worse than he is aware. In 2001, it was reported that unemployed Egyptian men were increasingly turning even to Israeli women for brides. Opposition MP Abul Aziz Al-Hariri complained to a parliamentary committee that Israel was encouraging the trend, and that rising unemployment was driving Egyptian men to such "desperate measures." News reports at the time quoted him as saying that, to escape the poverty trap, such men were marrying the Israeli women in ever greater numbers; he estimated that fourteen thousand Egyptian men had by that time married Israelis (although most are in fact Israeli Arabs of Palestinian descent). The same year, the second highest religious authority in Egypt proclaimed that it was sinful for an Egyptian to marry an Israeli. This kind of marriage, he explained, would help what he called Israel's plans to destroy the "Arab entity" and create generations of "potential spies" for Israel. More recently, the Egyptian magazine *Business Monthly* has pointed out that a clause in a new law limiting leases to ninety-nine years for those buying property in Sharm Al-Sheikh had been introduced as a direct result of a widely held belief that Israelis were buying up Sinai, which Israel occupied after the Six-Day War but returned to Egypt as part of the 1979 peace accords. A somewhat paranoid-sounding Egyptian real estate agent told the magazine: "A lot of the buyers had Jewish-looking names."

In reality, in Sharm Al-Sheikh, as in Luxor and other tourist cities (with the exception of Taba and other resorts in Sinai, where the majority of tourists are Israelis), it is British residential tourists who are growing in number faster than those of any other nationality, looking for investment, rental income, or just somewhere to escape the dreary English weather. Although there are no reliable statistics for total sales to foreigners in the Sharm Al-Sheikh area, *Business Monthly* gave a rough estimate based on figures obtained from four leading agencies. They indicated that foreigners bought at least three thousand units between 2004 and 2007. There, as in Luxor and the other main resort of Hurghada on the Red Sea, Egyptian men by the dozen sit along the waterfront blowing kisses at older women walking by, hoping that one of them will stop and say hello. At worst, a man will earn the equivalent of a month's wages by accompanying such a woman home for the night. At best, she will be looking for love, which he will declare from the bottom of his heart—so long as there is a visa to Britain as part of the bargain.

The reason Alaa was so fired up on the subject of foreign women that evening, it turned out, was that an article had appeared in the pan-Arab daily *Asharq Al-Awsat* a few days earlier, which he asked his wife to bring us from downstairs. As I read it through, he told me that everyone in the village had devoured its contents, and according to his friends the foreign women themselves were talking of little else on Luxor-themed Web sites that had posted English-language translations.

Local officials were quoted in the feature as saying that "the social makeup of Luxor will be drastically changed for the worse" if the new trend of local men marrying foreign women does not cease, and a new campaign would be launched to stress to young males the importance of marrying local Egyptian women. The local mayor acknowledged to the newspaper that the main motive behind such marriages was financial "rather than an expression of love," adding that the key to changing the situation lay in the creation of new and viable jobs for the young. He said such men totaled a staggering 40 percent of the city's total male population. The families of such men, he said, would prefer that their sons marry locally; but in light of the "difficult economic conditions" they nevertheless accepted that marrying a Western woman—"even if she may be as much as twice as old as their sons"—was an opportunity for social advancement too good to be passed up.

The report explained that strict local codes of conduct surrounding marriage and intermarriage were especially strong in Upper Egypt, as opposed to urban centers such as Cairo, where there is far more exposure to non-Egyptian cultural norms. Young people in Upper Egypt rarely date or spend time alone with one another prior to marriage. Instead, couples are paired up by matchmakers at early ages, with some girls being engaged by the age of nine or ten (though marriage under the age of fifteen is prohibited). Such matchmakers, along with parents, often choose a wife for a young male from his own family, where the woman's reputation, social status, and financial standing are clear. Cousins often marry on the condition that the male cousin is from the father's side, guaranteeing the continuation of the family name. "The new phenomenon of intermarriage with unknown, older foreign women is therefore extremely threatening to the traditional fabric of the community," *Asharq Al-Awsat* explained in this context, because "the preservation of lineage as well as local tradition for both men and women are maintained through local marriage custom." Additionally, as the number of young men who marry foreign women increases by the year, local women in Luxor are left with fewer options for entering a marriage and establishing a family, particularly since a large number of the men spend some time each year abroad with their foreign wives. "Time will tell whether the new trend will prove to be a temporary phenomenon, or a drastic new step away from tradition which may change Luxor society forever," the article concluded.

Unfortunately, *Asharq Al-Awsat,* which is Saudi-owned and thus shies away from direct criticism of the "brotherly" Egyptian regime, failed to note why such government-led campaigns aimed at changing the mind-set of the local youths have little chance of success: Corruption in the Luxor municipality seems as ingrained and unchecked as in many other government institutions in Egypt, and its apparent disregard for the well-being of the locals means there will be little chance the youth will escape the poverty trap by more legitimate means in the near future. This is a particularly shameful situation in a city where more than six million foreign visitors each year spend hundreds of millions of dollars, just a small percentage of which spent wisely could help alleviate many social ills. Instead, things are so dire that even the (chronically underfunded) local government hospital is casually referred to by locals as the Hospital of Death. The Western women, then, are a blessing as well as a curse, because they create a kind of surrogate welfare state for the masses of poor the government has no real interest in acknowledging, let alone improving the lot of. Also for political reasons, another subgroup the *Asharq Al-Awsat* article failed to mention are young Egyptian men trying to get out of compulsory military service, which lasts between six months and three years (depending on their level of education) and can pay as little as ten dollars a month. Egyptians married to foreigners are exempt from military service, again because of the perennial fear of "spies." Actually, it is technically illegal for anyone in the army even to befriend a foreign national, male or female, although that rule is not enforced in the foreigner-dominated tourist resorts, where it would take the resources of a whole army to implement it.

What bothered Alaa most, however, was the way his own personal social status had been reversed by these developments. Many of the men who were marrying foreigners, he claimed, were from the ranks of the illiterate, the lazy, or petty criminals (not that they are mutually exclusive groups). If true, that is a damning indictment of his fellow West Bankers, since he claims nearly all of them have married foreign women. Within days of meeting her, he continued, the young man is often given the equivalent of at least ten years of his own monthly salary of sixty-five dollars to buy land and build a villa, in addition to purchasing a brand-new car or motorcycle. A small business is usually also on the cards. Alaa could not help but laugh as he wondered aloud about the money some men were earning by having sex with foreign women. He asked if I remembered one such young man called Mohammed, who had worked at the budget hotel when Alaa was there bringing tourists from the airport and train station for a commission. I knew him well: He had bragged to me about how he was waiting for his own Big Opportunity, even boasting of how he wore no underwear beneath his tight white pants so that every foreign woman he encountered would immediately notice the outline of his huge, permanently semierect penis. Alaa told me that a month or so earlier Mohammed had finally gotten lucky: An English woman had taken the bait. He had already married her, and he now owned a taxi and a plot of land in another village on the West Bank, where they were planning to set up house.

"If I work all my life and save every penny, I'll never have what he now has," he said bitterly. "It's like the whole country: All the respectable people are on the bottom, and all the trash is at the top. When I was in school a teacher was the most respected man in the village. When he walked down the street, the pupils had to stand to one side to let him pass. Now they think you are pitiful if you're a teacher. They mock you for being too ugly or traditional to get a foreign wife."

It occurred to me, on hearing this last comment, that not a little of Alaa's frustration might in fact derive from jealousy rather than outrage: As someone not blessed with especially good looks, he had always been overlooked by the foreign women who perhaps attracted as much as repelled him. This hunch was confirmed next time I saw him, a few months after my first visit to his home. I had told him on the phone in advance that I was coming back down to Luxor from Cairo, but staying only a few days on my way to Aswan. His wife prepared us a wonderful meal. But from the outset Alaa seemed edgy. It turned out that he was preparing himself to ask me if I would "lend" him five thousand dollars to start a small business on the main road outside his village. Then he told me if I gave him an additional twenty thousand he would complete the second floor of his house, and let me stay upstairs for free whenever I was passing through. He mentioned these amounts as though he believed that for a foreigner like me they were negligible. I told him I would "think about it" and get back to him a few weeks later. The next day, I changed my cell phone number, and I never spoke to him again.

If he was prepared to try to take advantage of a friend in this way, how would he treat an older foreign woman if he married her?

Who are these older foreign women?

To generalize (and in the absence of in-depth anthropological studies, this is by necessity a generalization), many of those I bumped into during stays in Luxor and the many stories I heard about them from other Egyptians after my talk with Alaa indicated that a large number are English divorcees in their fifties or sixties, decent looking, and with only a basic education. While wealthy by local standards, they are typically living off minimal savings (for instance, the profit from an apartment sold back in England) and a state pension if (as is usually the case) they are old enough to be receiving one. The women who struck me as the most contented had accepted from the start that there was no possibility of love with the local men, and the relationship was essentially one of glorified prostitution. They took control of the situation, that is to say, and just made the most of the sex with handsome guys who would not look twice (or even once) at them back in England.

One such English woman I chatted with, who owned a business on the West Bank, still could not get over her luck, three years after moving to Luxor, at being showered with so much attention.

"My husband is much younger than me," she kept saying, rolling her eyes and tutting mischievously.

It was not difficult to see why she was so elated: Frankly, she looked like she had been run over by a London double-decker bus. Her Egyptian husband also had an Egyptian wife, so he would visit this British one only a few evenings a week, when he would give her a servicing and get a cash handout in return.

"He's very jealous of me," she said, rolling her eyes and tutting loudly again. This woman, though, was the exception.

So many more are in awful, mutually exploitative relationships with highly sophisticated con artists taking them for more than just a sexual ride. That the stories they tell, or that are told about them, are almost identical suggests that they have fallen into pretty much the same trap (in many instances even involving the same man). It would be unethical to give specific examples, and thus expose the women's private lives to public scrutiny, so I will say instead that their stories typically go something like this:

Initially she is flattered by the attention of an English-speaking young Egyptian man who, it appears, is by chance sitting by her table in a restaurant or walking alongside her in the street. After a chat, she agrees to go for a drink the following evening and during a stroll along the corniche afterward is taken in by his impassioned declarations of love. During the remainder of her holiday she weighs up the possibilities on offer here (lovely weather, great sex, luxury villa, cheap cost of living) to her life back home (fewer friends after the divorce, small apartment, great expenses, awful weather). She comes back to Egypt for an extended holiday, maybe a month or two, and marries the man who will help her start a new life (an *orfi* marriage entails little more getting a slip of paper officially stamped and signed). She gives him large sums of money so he can buy land and build their new home, but after she has been introduced to his dirt-poor family, who live in a godforsaken mud-hut village somewhere on the West Bank, she is emotionally blackmailed by sob stories about how his little brother needs money for schooling or his mother desperately requires cash for a lifesaving operation. Hooked on the sex, disoriented in a culture she has no experience of, and having abandoned her friends at home (maybe already having sold her apartment in England, too), she gives in time and again. The amounts being asked for are anyway relatively small compared to what she would have to pay in similar circumstances in England, she tells herself, and she is glad to be of help to such deserving, hospitable people. Over the months, though, the handouts are mounting and mounting; there is no end to the demands on her resources. Finally, she puts her foot down, after realizing she is being had, often after meeting other expatriate women (which her husband had done his best to keep her from coming into contact with) and hearing from them stories about how she is the tenth foreign wife this young man has "fallen in love with" in recent years, all of whom he has also milked dry. She tells him enough is enough. Within minutes, she is thrown out the door with just her suitcase; no one in her husband's house or the village that she had considered a model of hospitality just a few months before will now speak to her. She is told that she has been divorced. She books into a budget hotel because that is all she can afford, having lost everything she invested in (land, home, car, business) because he had conned her into having him sign all the contracts. Even if they are in her name, the Dickensian legal system means that, if she takes him to court, she will spend years if not decades trying to get a verdict; and if the verdict in the end does goes her way, she will have already spent more than she is awarded on bribing officials and paying highly inflated lawyer's fees—not having understood a thing that was going on anyway during the legal process because she does not know a word of Arabic. She usually decides, then, that it is better to cut her losses. After a few weeks of licking her wounds, she is out looking for another young Egyptian lover, and the whole ridiculous cycle begins again. She might even spot her former husband in a restaurant, where he just happens to be chatting to another older single Western woman: His hand is on her knee, he is staring deeply into her eyes . . .

That such marriages sometimes do not end even that amicably is a reality that can be attested to by Luxor tour guide Ibrahim Al-Sayyed Moussa, at present serving a fifteen-year prison sentence. He married a German woman, and the couple had three children; but when the marriage did not work out his wife suddenly left Egypt in 2001 and took the kids with her. When he discovered they were in Germany, he tried to join them, but the German embassy refused to grant him a visa. In a moment of madness, he kidnapped four German tourists in Luxor and tried to barter their release in exchange for his children. The hostages were released, and he was carted off to jail.

Of course, not all such cross-cultural marriages in Luxor are abysmal failures. But all the anecdotal evidence available suggests that a lot of them are. It is difficult in any case to think they are viable in the long term: If the

man is twenty-five and the woman sixty-five when they marry, who can seriously believe they will still be together fifteen years later, when he is forty and she is eighty?

Single Western women traveling through or studying in Egypt, and Western women who have met and married Egyptian men in more normal circumstances (as fellow students at college, say, or as work colleagues in the same office), deeply resent these English grannies who prowl the streets of Luxor, Sharm Al-Sheikh, Hurghada, and other resorts in search of street meat. The reason is that they tend to give all Western women a reputation for being fair game, even though it is technically the Egyptian men who are the prostitutes since they are the ones who are paid for their services.

But the wider ramifications only begin there: Even Western men who accompany their Western wives to Egypt can find themselves fuming at the unwanted attention directed her way, and not just in Luxor. Egyptians from all over the country, after all, travel to work in the tourist resorts, and the reputation of older foreign females has hit rock bottom throughout the country. Altercations are commonplace. Sometimes, the consequences can be deadly.

In a bizarre reversal of the "cultural contamination" theory, for example, an Englishman was jailed for life in 2007 after committing what can only be described as an "honor killing" by bludgeoning his English wife to death. The reason was her affair with a younger man she met when they went on holiday together to Egypt. Fifty-three-year-old Ron Johnson, according to the British tabloid *The Daily Express,* flipped because his forty-nine-year-old wife, Sue, had fallen for an Egyptian taxi driver fifteen years her junior. The jury heard how the couple had booked their two-week trip to Egypt to console themselves and revive their thirty-two-year marriage after plans to retire to Cyprus had fallen through. They hired a certain Saad Elembaby to show them around, and Johnson quickly became enraged at seeing the younger man flirting with his receptionist wife. They would, he said, "dodge behind monuments for secret kisses." When the three of them galloped across desert sands on horses, Johnson was said to "cut a sad, sidelined figure." He told police that Saad "was always trying to keep close to Sue, touchy and feely. I kept saying, 'Oi, she's *my* wife.' He replied, jokingly, that he would slit my throat." His wife was having what was called a midlife crisis, or a "Shirley Valentine moment," as the *Daily Express* put it, and she found his behavior "very flattering." After the holiday, the pair exchanged texts and e-mails, and Mrs. Johnson returned briefly to Egypt, telling her husband that when Elembaby touched her it was like "an electric shock." After her return to the family home in Nottinghamshire, Johnson smashed his sleeping wife's skull with a hammer, and then stabbed her with a knife for good measure. Afterward, he tried to kill himself by downing painkillers, hanging himself with a dog's leash, and piercing his neck with an electric drill. He survived, though, and was given a twelve-year sentence.

It cuts both ways, then. Older Western women ignorant of or just not very concerned about local traditions do appear to be undermining the social fabric of Upper Egypt's conservative tribal culture. But Egyptian men would do well to learn that they should treat others as they would be treated themselves. For many of them, too, are also steeped in ignorance when it comes to the question of how older Western women normally behave, based on generalizations in light of the relatively small number who are on the lookout for a bit of "touchy, feely."

Then there is the more blatant hypocrisy: The Egyptian taxi driver who seduced Mrs. Johnson would surely not merely joke about "slitting

the throat" of any man who as much as hinted he was interested in sleeping with his own Egyptian wife.

If single Western women travelers have a hard time in Luxor, it is as nothing as compared to what single Western men have to suffer.

Growing numbers of Western gay sex tourists have discovered that Luxor is billed as a gay hotspot by gay-themed international Web sites. Ostensibly promoting the alien Western concept of "gay rights" in a country where only a tiny, Westernized, urban "gay" elite can or would ever want to relate to it, the Web sites concentrate more heavily on providing up-to-the-minute information to Western gay men looking for paid sex with locals.

The older foreign women who commented on their own Luxor-themed Web sites that reprinted the *Asharq Al-Awsat* article were, I later discovered when I read through them, eager to point out in this context that it was not just they who were to blame for the growth of male prostitution in the city. Why, they wanted to know, were the gay Westerners who also flock to Luxor not being singled out? The reason, of course, is that since the subject is taboo in Arabic-language public forums, the *Asharq Al-Awsat* journalist would have had no choice but to steer well clear of it. Alas, while bringing up this relevant related topic, many of the Web site comments by the foreign women went beyond rational discussion and instead adopted a brutish—one is tempted to write British—tone, damning without qualification what they referred to as "promiscuous" Western gays who sleep with local youths during their brief holidays, who were "corrupting" the young and "undermining local traditions" in a way they themselves could never be accused of doing. Inevitably, the hysteria about pedophilia that continues to whip the British tribal working classes into a frenzy also entered the discussion. Some participants even suggested that they should start picketing apartments that the men with a penchant for youths are known to rent, although no evidence was offered that any of them had any interest in children. This overreaction was a predictable example, it struck me, of a marginalized social group feeling the heat from the mainstream, and so deflecting attention away from themselves by trying to demonize a smaller, even more vulnerable one.

Anyway, the reality is that, unlike sex between young men and older women, sex with and between youths is very much part of the Luxor social fabric, and it has been so since time immemorial. What takes precedence in Upper Egypt is always tribal norms and customs: Even the saint-worshiping Sufi form of Islam that is practiced in the region plays second fiddle to tribalism. You can count the number of Muslim Brotherhood supporters in Luxor on one hand. The Saudi-funded *Asharq Al-Awsat* newspaper, which promotes the Wahhabi agenda endorsed by the House of Saud, did not feel compelled even obliquely to make the case that sex tourism might "undermine Islam" in the region.

Tribal custom dictates that women's honor must be protected at all costs, and in the absence of other opportunities for sex before marriage homosexuality is seen as an acceptable trade-off. The golden rule, though, is that it should not be discussed or conducted in ways that might draw attention, and thus create a scandal, and that a boy should be careful not to get a reputation for enjoying the passive role, for if he does he will be considered a slut, lose his own honor and suffer the consequences of his friends thinking they have the right to screw him whenever they get the urge. This is not to say that, in relation to the impact of the influx of foreign gay men, the gay prostitution phenomenon is not a "chicken and the egg" issue. In reading through the older foreign women's homophobic comments on their Luxor-theme Web sites, I was reminded of an amusing exchange I overheard between a Yemeni and an American in Saudi Arabia. The American had mocked tribal Yemenis as notorious pederasts.

"Yes, we learned about boy love from the English," the Yemeni quipped.

"Oh no, the English decided to stay on and colonize the country only after they discovered it was so widespread!" the American shot back.

One day in the souk where I used to hang out in Luxor a tall, handsome lad about sixteen years old appeared wearing new clothes, sporting a new haircut, and listening to his favorite local singer on a new MP3 player (when not chatting to a friend on the latest Nokia cell phone). After preening himself in a mirror in one of the shop windows he sat down in the coffee shop at a table near my own and invited his pals to have a soft drink. They settled down to a game of backgammon.

"Who is he?" one of them teased him after a few minutes.

"He's from England," the boy replied.

"How long is he here for?" another wanted to know.

"Two weeks. But he's already been here for a week, so he's leaving after another."

"Has he been here before?" a third lad asked.

"Yes, this is his second time. He lives in Alexandria, but he's thinking of moving here next year."

"Is he going to buy you a motorbike?" he was pressed.

"God willing, he will. But I haven't asked him yet," he said matter-of-factly.

I sipped my tea and continued to read the newspaper. Like the locals who were also listening to the exchange, I had heard the same kind of talk more times than I cared to remember. That such a conversation could be held in the full public glare might strike many in the West as odd, to say the least, since the perception is that the Arab world, and Egypt in particular, is deeply homophobic. But since he is assumed to be the active partner in the relationship with the self-defined "gay" foreigner, or at least not the passive partner, the boy suffers no stigma as a result of his admission, and as an outsider the foreigner is not expected to conform to local norms and values. Locals even refer to the older foreign women as "gay" because, for them, the label is given only to an individual—male or female—who takes the passive sexual role.

So there is no Western-style gay bashing here, and no organized persecution, because among the locals there is no Western-style concept of being exclusively "gay" in the sense of choosing to "live a gay lifestyle"—something completely anathema even to the most enthusiastic local boy enthusiasts because it threatens the all-important tribal hierarchy. As long as his older Western friend is in town, the only pressure the boy will face is constant pleading from friends to take them with him to the foreigner's apartment, or to liberally spread his newfound wealth around.

While older foreign women in relationships with young men have the legal cover of an *orfi* marriage, the gay Westerner has the social cover of "friendship" in an exclusively male environment to justify his entanglement with the youth. Not that he will be asked to justify himself. What they get up to behind closed doors is nobody's business. As long as the locals are not children, who are fiercely protected and adored, it would be shameful (and illegal) for a local to try to make an issue of the relationship, and if he insisted on doing so he would likely create an eternal feud between the youth's family and his own. Discretion, then, is the name of the game. Moreover, while the boy may be from a poor family, there are no starving, homeless, glue-sniffing kids in Luxor of the kind unfortunately exploited by sex tourists in other Arab countries such as Morocco and Tunisia. So if the youth did not want to go to the Western man's apartment, the reasoning ultimately seems to be, he simply would not go; and the best thing therefore is to leave well enough alone, and let him be taken care of financially.

Such Western men, historically attracted to the Arab world partly because they find the gay-liberation-era ghettos in the West reductive and stifling, are often introduced to the families of their kept youths, where they are referred to as his "uncle." A number of such friendships in Luxor have lasted a great many years, continuing even after the boy has grown up and gotten married.

If things always played out in this quiet fashion, one might be tempted even to praise the liberalism and tolerance the relationships represent, not least since Arabs are so often portrayed in the West as sexually prudish and repressed. But if Nasser's gift to the Egyptians was their sense of pride, Mubarak's curse is to have created a cultural climate where the only rewarded character traits are shameless opportunism and lack of dignity. In a country where the fat cats are robbing the country blind, and where scandals about how ministers have siphoned off tens of millions of dollars into foreign bank accounts are routine, stealing and swindling are seen as the only way to get ahead.

In Luxor these days, what was once a tastefully hidden but widespread pederastic phenomenon has therefore been firmly dragged out of the closet and commercialized as a result of the gay foreigner influx. Now any single Western man, whether he likes boys or not, soon discovers that living a normal life in Luxor is well nigh impossible. At least half of the local youths would, without a second thought, sell their bodies to a Western man, and many of them do so on a regular basis, the only condition being that they are not expected to perform the passive role.

Sit in a coffee shop where you are not known, and within minutes you will be surrounded by local youths wanting to know if you are married and, if they discover you are not, asking whether you would like to take one of them back to your apartment. Go to the local public swimming pool and the teens walking past will gesture at their lower bodies with a filthy smirk: an invitation to give them a blow job, for the right price. Tuned into the latest tourism trends, they all know about the gay-themed Web sites and the places preposterously listed on them as "gay cruising areas" (as though there is anywhere in Luxor *not* a gay cruising area). If you happen to pass by one of these venues, it is immediately assumed that you are looking for a pickup. Even if you tell the leering and jeering boys to take a run and a jump in Arabic, at least one (and usually more) will follow you for what feels like an eternity in the hope that sooner or later you will turn and make conversation. If you rent an apartment, you had better tell the door-man on the first day that under no circumstances is he to let anyone in who claims to be a friend, otherwise there will be a constant thundering on the door from a succession of youths, each trying his luck.

The authorities seem to spring into action only when pornography is involved, literally threatening as it does to "tarnish Egypt's image abroad." But I could discover just two incidents where the police had become involved. One involved a Westerner who had moored his yacht on the Nile and then had dozens of local youths have sex with him inside it while they took photographs, some of which later found their way into the hands of a member of the tourist police (in addition to the rest of the local population; almost everyone I mentioned this to on the corniche after first hearing about it claimed to have seen the pictures, and one even offered to get me copies if I was prepared to pay). The other was a Westerner unknowingly photographed by a boy using a cell phone camera while having sex in his apartment with some of the boy's friends, and who afterward tried to extort money from him by threatening to post them on the Web. Amazingly, he complained to the tourist police, who arrested the boys but also asked the foreigner to leave the country on the next plane. (Sail from the country, or at least the city, is what they told the guy with the yacht to do as well.) Nobody I talked to knew what punishment, if any, the youths themselves had been given. The consensus was that they were probably just given a beating and then let go.

This, then, is the "gay-friendly" city advertised on Web sites that now draw hundreds, perhaps thousands, of Western gay men to Luxor every year. Given these large numbers, not a few of them sadly turn out to be as shameless as the locals (why would the latter always expect the worst otherwise?), and in July 2007 one particular individual's antics became the talk of the town. His behavior illustrates how the growth of gay male prostitution could indeed have terrible consequences for Luxor's next generation. The elderly Englishman, who had been visiting Egypt for years, was suffering from AIDS and had recently been told by his doctor that he had only a short time to live. He decided that he wanted to be screwed into the grave, and he chose Luxor as his final resting place. During his final few weeks, his local pimp brought him at least a dozen local youths every day. They sodomized him, one after the other, without wearing condoms. When this man's foreign friend, who was also gay but in a long-term relationship with a local, got wind of what was happening, he threatened to inform the police; but he was initially reassured by his friend that he was indeed practicing safe sex. Unconvinced, he asked the pimp directly, who told him that the local youths never used condoms, either when they have sex with one another or with Westerners (unless the latter insists), and in this instance the Westerner did not insist. Outraged, he decided to turn his friend in to the police. But he was robbed of the opportunity when the AIDS carrier, after telling his pimp he wanted to go to sleep after being sodomized by about the tenth young man that day, never woke up.

His Egyptian "friends" subsequently held a party in his honor. And it turned out that he had left his considerable inheritance to the pimp himself. To add insult to injury, his ashes were later scattered in the Nile by his sister. She had been accompanying her brother on trips to Luxor for years.

Edgar in *King Lear* says:

The worst is not
So long as we can say,
"This is the worst."

It is a quotation that should be written on the main entrance into the city of Luxor. Even worse than the incident itself was that everyone knew what was happening before the man died, not just the locals but the police as well. With their extensive network of secret informants, the police know everything that is going on in the city, particularly among those who rent private apartments because their main informants are the doormen who guard the entrances. Even I had found out about him two or three days before he died, when I had a drink with a friend.

"Every time I see him walking in the street I say in a loud voice: 'May Allah take this man away from us! May Allah take this man who is killing our youth!'" he told me.

He lost his temper when I advised him to tell the tourism police.

"Are you completely stupid?" he spat out with uncharacteristic rudeness. "They will arrest me for causing trouble! And the boys will just say they are his friends and deny they had sex with him. Then what will I do? They will gang up on me. And the police are all taking kickbacks from the pimp: a packet of cigarettes here, a few Egyptian pounds there. You just can't complain about anything a foreigner does. Even if you beat me up now for no reason, the police will arrest me and ask if you are okay. You Westerners have impunity."

This man was an exception in that he was outraged. Almost all the local youths I talked to about what had happened after the foreigner died responded by laughing, calling the boys who had visited him "donkeys" and saying they deserved their fate if they knew he had AIDS.

It was only after witnessing this callousness firsthand that I began to understand in retrospect the national reaction to the arrest of an alleged serial killer of small boys in December 2006. Ahmed Abdul Rahmin Mansour, a twenty-six-year-old gang leader from a town north of Cairo, murdered more than thirty street boys and was also charged with their kidnapping, rape, and torture. His four-man gang's seven-year reign of terror extended over several provinces, and he confessed before identifying twelve of his victims from photographs. Mansour earned the nickname "Al-Turbiny," from the air-conditioned express trains linking Cairo with Egypt's second city Alexandria, whose roofs were the favored location for his crimes. Police said he would to rape, torture, and chop up his victims on carriage roofs before tossing them on to the trackside, dead or barely alive.

Astonishingly, *Al-Ahram*, the main state-owned newspaper, later reported that Egyptian products were now being named after Al-Turbiny. Restaurants in the Nile Delta city of Tanta, the newspaper said, were doing "a roaring trade" in a new so-called Al Turbiny sandwich, "while sheep traders are also exploiting the name as a mark of their beasts' pedigree."

Perhaps the "strangest such marketing ploy," *Al-Ahram* said, was that of owners of communications centers and supermarkets in the Nile Delta town of Gharbia were renaming their businesses "Al-Turbiny: The Butcher of Gharbia," "butcher" being a colloquial pun on the word "leader." This reaction borders on the incomprehensible, but what it clearly indicates is that something has gone terribly wrong with contemporary Egyptian society.

One thing not difficult to understand, though, is the reason foreigners are indulged: Egypt received a record 9.7 million visitors in 2006–2007, a 13 percent increase over the 8.6 million in the previous year, and they spent $8.2 billion (an increase of 14 percent on the $7.2 billion in the previous year).

While religion is not an especially key element in the lives of most Egyptians who live in Luxor, Islamists of course see the city and the wider tourism industry in the broader context of their bid to cleanse Egypt of foreign cultural influences. It was no coincidence that the most spectacular and tragic terrorist attack carried out in the country's recent history occurred in the West Bank of Luxor at Hatshepsut Temple. In 1997, dozens of Egyptians and tourists were massacred at the site. But as early as 1990 an employee had thrown a Molotov cocktail into a restaurant on the edge of the Red Sea, killing a German man and French woman and severely burning a number of others. The terrorist claimed that the tourists were "offending Islam" by their behavior. Tourists had bombs thrown at them in Luxor in 1992 in similar circumstances, and at the time a leader of the terror group behind these and a whole series of other attacks said that "tourism must be hit because it is corrupt" and "brings alien customs and morals that offend Islam."

CHAPTER EIGHT

EGYPT AFTER MUBARAK

Luxor is both an exhilarating and deeply depressing city: the majesty of the monuments and of the civilization of which they are a reminder contrast with the crass commercialization, from the highest to the lowest levels, that is parasitic of the past and corrupting of the present. The Egyptians are understandably proud of the legacy and state with pride that it enables them to take the long view. But it has to be said that there may be no long term, at least for the present regime, if important and pressing issues are not addressed in the short term. That the short term promises to be uneasy became clear in September 2007, when rumors began to circulate in Cairo that Hosni Mubarak was gravely ill, possibly even dead. Soon vaguely sourced stories began to appear on the front pages of opposition newspapers. There was an almost wishful quality to their tone. That was unsurprising: Barely a day had gone by since the new opposition media came out of its shell in 2003 in the wake of the U.S.-led invasion of Iraq—when the Bush administration briefly encouraged the promise of promoting democracy in the wider Arab world and Egyptian liberals enjoyed a "Cairo Spring" as a result—that did not see the front pages of the opposition press hurling insults at Mubarak and son, Gamal. Most Egyptians, it was clear, wanted to be rid of the Mubarak dynasty, with the exceptions only of the regime's hangers-on. While the regime had cracked down on dissent in the interim, no one I met during the weeks when it was thought Mubarak was on his deathbed expressed even the vaguest kind of sympathy for him. The swirl of unsubstantiated rumor and official denial were indicative of a mixture of hope, fear, and most especially uncertainty—for in the absence of legitimate government and regularized routines for succession, speculation and conjecture were the name of the game.

Yet however much Mubarak and his regime have alienated the Egyptians, the possibility of his leaving the scene did not generate any sense of elation—or even any relief. Rather, the widespread sense of disgust at his legacy combined with a resignation about what would come in his wake. Everyone took for granted that Gamal would by hook or by crook ascend to the presidency. That such a succession had happened in Syria and Morocco, and appeared in the offing in Libya, gave credence to the speculation, despite repeated official denials. That Gamal seemed to many woefully unprepared for the task, whether due to his perceived shortcomings or to the failure of the regime adequately to lay the groundwork, only raised anxiety that a bumpy transition would lead to instability with unknown and undesired outcomes. That the devil one knows may be better than the unknown was clear when, paradoxically, it turned out that the health scare was based only on gossip, and the regime moved swiftly to silence its opponents.

The subsequent regime crackdown on dissent targeted the editors in chief who had printed stories about Mubarak's health, rights groups who were publishing increasingly bold reports about torture and corruption, and political opposition movements such as the Muslim Brotherhood (dozens of whose members, including a top leader, were already on trial in a military court on what were viewed as trumped-up charges, including terrorism and money laundering). Four journalists were subsequently handed jail terms for defaming the president; an editor was sent to trial for reporting on the Mubarak health rumors; and, for the first time ever, the Muslim Brotherhood was even barred from hosting its annual Ramadan dinner. Ayman Nour, who stood against Mubarak in a presidential election and received a five-year jail sentence shortly afterwards, was nearing death in his prison cell, while the pro-democracy reformer Saad Eddin Ibrahim said he feared being tortured and killed if he set foot in Egypt after calling from abroad for greater accountability and democracy, even alleging in an interview that the regime had set up a death squad to bump off opponents (a claim no one has proven). In moving against its critics in this way, the regime silenced discussion of Mubarak's health. More to the point, the speculation and anxiety had perhaps made clear to the regime that, if succession was to be Gamal's, now was not quite the moment.

All the speculation about and attention to Mubarak's health and Gamal's future role had the further ironic effect of keeping attention away from the reality of Egyptian power, and the opposition was as complicit, perhaps unwittingly, as the regime. The president, that is to say, is a figurehead who conducts the messy, day-to-day business of governing the country, while the real power, the military establishment, rules behind the scenes. In Egypt, as Steven A. Cook of the Council on Foreign Relations has pointed out, the Egyptian armed forces "have declared many sectors of the economy under its control—by no means confined to military production—strictly off-limits to privatization." Egypt's military establishment, Cook adds, "owns such businesses as the Safi spring-water company, aviation services, security services, travel services, footwear production, and kitchen-appliance manufacturing." He might have added something about all the land and shopping malls they own, too.

The military regime has played its cards very shrewdly, ruling but not governing. Very little of importance gets done in Egypt without the military and the security services at the least being aware, usually taking a cut of the pie; and certainly very little, if anything, is done that threatens their position. The military is by no means the all-dominant power it was in the 1950s and 1960s, and the phenomenal growth of the internal security forces means it now acts as a counterweight to the military's power; but the military remains a crucial pillar, many would argue *the* crucial pillar, of the regime. Former military officers are well entrenched in the government as cabinet ministers, the heads of public sector companies, and provincial governors. But if the opposition media had focused its attention where it really mattered, and shone a light on the corruption amongst the military behind the figurehead of the president, the crackdown they would have provoked would have made the one launched in the wake of the Mubarak health scare seem like a mere sideshow. It is commonly understood in Egypt that criticism is allowed, but is limited; the president, until very recently, was off limits, and criticism of the military regime remains out of bounds.

Some have argued that the rise of Gamal, who as head of the powerful Policies Secretariat has been the driving force behind the privatization of the economy, promises a breath of fresh air, modernizing and opening up the economy. Those hopes are balanced by concerns that doing such has the potential to create a schism within the regime, with unforeseen consequences. The most optimistic observers suggest that a more competitive economic system in Egypt will create significant splits within the capitalist class and thus lead to wider political pluralism representing different economic interests, even including those of the workers. But this is all wishful thinking. One need only look at the similar hopes, since dashed, after Hafez Al-Assad was succeeded by his so modern, Western-educated, cosmopolitan son Bashar. Years later, the Syrian regime is all the more isolated, accused of sponsoring terrorism and accused of murdering a Lebanese prime minister, having close ties to Iran, and being as tediously intolerant of differing points of view at home as ever. In Syria, the power behind the presidential throne reasserted itself, and whatever Bashar's personal inclinations, his room for maneuver was severely constrained as a consequence. If Gamal does indeed take over from his father, he, too, will do so only with the consent of the military, on the understanding that his privatization drive especially will not undermine their considerable perks, and that they will continue to call the shots in terms of foreign policy, where they work closely with America and as a result continue to receive $2 billion in military aid. The only chance of a rupture is if Mubarak decides to push Gamal toward the presidency *despite* objections put forward by the military. The reason the military may object is that Gamal, unlike Nasser, Al-Sadat, and Mubarak himself, is not from within their own military ranks. Some point to the possibility of a military coup in such circumstances. However, the different branches of Egypt's dictator class are, as we have seen, deeply entwined, and their collective concern is first and foremost their own survival. So compromise is far more likely than confrontation, especially at a time of domestic upheaval, when any appearance of weakness or vulnerability must be avoided at all costs.

All the hopes and indeed fears placed on the fragile shoulders of Gamal are rather curious, given how little he has actually done, though of course his lack of achievements makes him something of a cipher: People read into him what they will. Much attention has been paid to his symbolic achievements, consistent with a long tradition of verbiage replacing achievement as a criterion for leadership. For example, at the 2006 National Democratic Party conference, Gamal dropped a bombshell by announcing that the country would seek to develop nuclear power, a symbol of modernity, which if pursued would be costly, a long time in coming, and geared to aggravate the Americans (given their concerns about proliferation in the region). Following a nationally televised address by Gamal, who is also the deputy secretary-general of the NDP, a government body called the Supreme Council for Energy created a committee made up of five ministries—including those of electricity and energy, gasoline and defense—to further explore the nuclear option. The body has since convened for the first time since Egypt's original nuclear program was publicly shelved by Mubarak in 1986, following the accident at the Soviet nuclear plant in Chernobyl. The new push on the nuclear energy front was reinforced by the president himself during his conference-closing speech, in which he stated that Egypt "must benefit from sources of new and renewable energy, including peaceful uses of nuclear energy." That the announcement was more about posturing and promises than pragmatics became clear at a separate meeting on the sidelines of the NDP conference, where Gamal told foreign journalists that Egypt would no longer adhere to Bush's democracy initiatives in the Middle East. This was perceived as a calculated effort to raise the younger Mubarak's profile and show defiance toward the United States. He also reportedly said U.S. policies in the region had provided a fertile breeding ground for extremism. "We reject visions from abroad that attempt to undermine Arab identity and joint Arab efforts," he said, and in a clear message to the White House included "the so-called Greater Middle East Initiative" among those foreign visions. *The New York Times* noted that distancing himself from

Washington and the pursuit of nuclear power are actions that could help counteract two of the younger Mubarak's perceived shortcomings as a possible successor to his father, namely, that he would be the first president since the coup ousted the monarchy who is not a military officer and that both he and his father are often perceived as tools of Washington. The nuclear program might, that is to say, help him win support among the military, and the swipes at Washington might help him win some credibility with the public. Both moves were probably intended to co-opt a policy that the government assumed would go down well with the public, and thus possibly build a popular consensus around the figure of the president's son. But they are clutching at straws. If the goal was to give greater credibility to Gamal, the strategy was a failure: As the events surrounding the president's supposed illness indicated, Gamal remains as hated as ever by the masses; and Egypt remains just as beholden to the United States. The proposed nuclear program, meanwhile, has remained moribund; anyway, Washington swiftly endorsed it, thus cleverly nipping in the bud Gamal's attempts at orchestrated confrontation.

Not that Gamal is a complete lightweight. There is evidence that he is both aware of the need for change, of the challenges posed by the opposition, especially the Muslim Brotherhood, and able to draw on professionals who may be able to initiate and even implement change—albeit within the strict limits of a presidency that rules but does not govern. One example of those whom Gamal has surrounded himself with is Hossam Badrawi, a businessman and one of his closest confidants. He chairs the Education and Scientific Research Committee of the Policies Secretariat, of which Gamal is the chairman, and he has been mentioned as getting the health or education portfolio if Gamal does become president. U.S.-educated, he is also a member of the Policies Secretariat's Higher Policies Council, the brainchild of the National Democratic Party's legislative proposals and reforms. In addition, he serves in his private capacity as chairman of Nile Badrawi Hospital and of Middle East Medicare, the country's first and as yet only health maintenance organization. With a chain of forty private hospitals, this HMO provides services that the state has failed to, and in a sense stands as a counter to the Muslim Brotherhood's similar attempts to gain support through providing welfare where the state has failed. Badrawi is unique among members of the NDP in that he is genuinely popular, largely because he is seen as anticorruption but also because he has a self-effacing manner. His popularity lay behind a decision by NDP bigwigs to unseat him from the Qasr Al-Nil district of Cairo in 2005. The decision to deny him a role in parliament represented the power of the establishment. That Badrawi kept all his NDP committee positions represented the power of Gamal. In may ways, then, his experiences and views represent the tough middle ground that Gamal and his supporters have to navigate.

I met with Badrawi in October 2006 in the top-floor office of his flagship hospital in the upscale Cairo distinct of Maadi, a hospital as efficiently run and state-of-the-art as any you will find in the West. That he is aware of what needs to be done to drag Egypt into the twenty-first century is clear, given his activities. For example, one of the most pressing issues facing Egypt is the education of its youth. Historically, the educational establishment has been bloated and inefficient, with instruction driven by rote and mimicry rather than inquisitiveness. That is hardly surprising, given the authoritarian nature of the regime, and that during the Nasser period those who went along to get along knew that their obedience would be repaid with a government job where little initiative was expected. To be sure, the low pay was far from ideal, and the government got what it paid for: inefficiency, red tape, and corruption. But eventually the bloated bureaucracy became a burden, and assured employment was eliminated. The educational system had yet to adjust. Badrawi had been involved with NDP studies on education, yet found that "none of the recommendations that we proposed as policies were later implemented on the micro level." He is an eager backer of the Education for Employment Foundation, which works to ease unemployment in the Islamic world by creating career training schools in partnership with local businesses; the difference in its vision from that of the state's is encapsulated in his noting that "one of the most important policies in education is to connect people to employment" in the private sector; that is, students need to gain the skills and frames of mind that will be beneficial in a competitive environment. The importance of this training was more pressing than creating jobs, he said, "for the jobs were there; the problem is the employability of the people coming out of the education system. We have a mass of unemployed people who are also unemployable. They do not graduate with enough knowledge, they are not competitive, and they do not have an entrepreneurial spirit. Everyone is just waiting for someone to employ them."

This tendency toward passivity and a desire—indeed, expectation—that others will provide is, alas, all too prevalent in Egypt. One of the legacies of Nasser's socialism has been that competition was disparaged; one of the legacies of Al-Sadat's opening up was that competition was not to create and innovate, but rather to gain favor from the state. There is a famous Egyptian joke: At every fork in the road Nasser went left, Al-Sadat went right, and Mubarak says, "Don't move." The result is the worst of all worlds, and hence Egypt's stagnation. There are, of course, those who benefit from the system, and these are the people who seek to impede innovators like Badrawi. As he noted, he lost his parliamentary seat "because my own party was fighting against me, and the reason is that they are fighting against reform." Given what happened, his faith that reform can come from within is curious, to say the least. But he is, he said, "trying to create within the party what we call a critical mass of political power that's genuinely pushing for reform." Evidence for success comes so far from "changing the language of everyone. They may not mean what they say, but at least everyone is talking about equality, standards, democracy, transparency, performance, evaluation. . . . At the same time, this has made the situation more difficult, because if you sit with someone and he says he agrees on all the principles but then does something else, you really don't know what to do. Now we are fighting corruption and hypocrisy at the same time!"

Whatever his ties to Gamal, Badrawi says that while he supports him, the important thing is "our work should concentrate on having the integrity of elections rather than speaking about individuals. If we have free elections, then any party and indeed anyone should be able to nominate candidates. If Gamal is a candidate for the NDP, he will be a candidate as anyone else could be, including myself." That Gamal is a reformer and has both sponsored and protected reformers is clear to Badrawi, as his own experiences indicate; after all, given his openness to interacting with the opposition, including the Muslim Brotherhood, he would not be able to maintain his position in the absence of some protection. His call for free elections is encouraging. But one has to wonder what his colleagues in the NDP think about his observation that "I know—and they know—that reform will entail losing power. What I'm telling my party is that part of the process of reform is indeed losing part of the power."

And when one dives through all the proclamations, verbiage, promises, stoking of fears of Islamist takeover, that is the rub: No one in power wants to lose it. And if you have power, even giving up part of it involves the danger of an uncontrollable spiral. The Egyptian regime came to power through a coup, on the crest of rioting that had the potential to get out of control—perhaps even bring the Muslim Brotherhood to power. For whatever reason, the coup leaders let King Farouk abdicate and go into exile, to be forgotten by history until the situation in Egypt got so bad that he became an object of nostalgia. Not every deposed leader is so fortunate. Here is the catch–22: Opening up and allowing competition risks losing control, but stifling dissent risks creating pent-up frustrations that will eventually either necessitate a massive crackdown or cause an explosion that is uncontrollable and potentially disastrous—for both the regime and the people. Badrawi told me frankly that "there is no trust between the government and the people," and that basic fact bodes ill. Those at the top in favor of the status quo have no faith in the people, and they point to discontent and violence as evidence that, absent a stern hand, danger lurks.

Such beliefs are resistant to change and readily grasp at evidence that the people are a tinderbox. Recent events may even strengthen this perception. During the spring and summer of 2007 there were hundreds of wildcat strikes in various industries, a wave of industrial unrest involving tens of thousands of workers on a scale not seen in Egypt since the years leading up to the coup in 1952. By wildcat I mean not authorized by the official and government-controlled labor union. The union itself is a legacy of Nasser's day, when state-controlled industry was protected from external competition through a variety of means; the result, needless to say, was massive inefficiencies, waste, and featherbedding, all used as a means to tie the people to the government. For a long time there has been talk of liberalization and privatization; indeed, these are two pillars of the reformers' plans. But the net effect is to threaten the workers, who in turn pose a far greater threat to the regime than the embattled liberal opposition activists gathered around newspapers (which only a tiny elite read) and political parties prone to official harassment and seemingly endless and usually petty infighting.

Not surprisingly, the workers had limited tolerance of stagnant wages eroded by inflation combined with the potential of losing their jobs. With "their" union defenders alleged to be in cahoots with the regime, eventually their patience ran out. That the workers' demonstrations tended to be sporadic, uncoordinated, and localized could have been of only small comfort to the regime. For the stalwarts it provided a boon: they could point to the demonstrations as indicating the very serious risk—should they become more widespread and coordinated and make more than immediate, economic demands—of rebellion; and at the same time, they could argue that the reformers were therefore doubly responsible, first by calling for privatization (which the workers resent) and second by calling for political reform (which gave the workers confidence and, crucially, the oxygen of press coverage in the opposition media). For the stalwarts the preference is neither: The status quo of protecting the people while stifling them is better than the risks of economic or political reform, let alone both at the same time. One can certainly understand that position, as misguided as it obviously is.

Egypt is not the first, and will not be the last, country to face this conundrum. Since the 1990s there have been two general models: that of the Soviet Union, and that of China. Roughly, the Soviet model was to try to open the way to reform both politically and economically at the same time, with, if anything, the former ahead of the latter. The result was hardly reassuring to authoritarian regimes: The Soviet Union disintegrated, and the ruling elite lost power. The Chinese model, on the other hand, looks more attractive: Economic openness was encouraged, while political openness was limited, and when there was a threat of the party losing power, it crushed the opposition. Whether this strategy will work in the long term, meaning that the party retains power, remains an open question.

But there are a number of important differences between Egypt, on the one hand, and either the former Soviet Union or China, on the other. For one thing, both of the latter regimes based their rule on an ideology that gave a sense of reason and rationale, that people could in some form believe in. The Soviet and Chinese communist parties were also deeply ingrained in their societies, and there were considerable incentives to conform and awful punishments for dissent. And both the Soviets and the Chinese could point to considerable achievements, even as the atrocities each regime committed over time were covered up and hidden from the people—at least officially. Of the many things that distinguish the Soviet and Chinese cases, two may be pointed to: First, for little-understood reasons the elite of the Soviet Union seemed to lose their faith and become divided among themselves, which allowed outsiders increasingly to challenge, and ultimately overthrow, the regime; second, the Chinese were better able to change the nature of the relationship with the people by more quickly providing economic benefits and hope for improvement.

The truly awful thing about the Mubarak regime is just how bankrupt it is, as it muddles aimlessly along. There is no ideological rationale that it offers, no standards to which the people can be rallied. Pan-Arabism long ago was jettisoned; Islam is the solution proffered by the opposition. While there have been improvements in the economy, their distribution has been so uneven and skewed toward those affiliated with the regime that resentment and resignation have, if anything, increased. The regime's political party has no real links to the people, and outside the major cities is barely a presence. In short, Mubarak's regime has none of the attributes that kept either the Soviets or the Chinese Communist parties in power. It has no reason for being, other than to cling to power.

In the absence of any kind of legitimacy, what keeps it in power is therefore fear. The everyday violence that permeates the society through the thugs in the police and the only slightly more adroit security services are a basic form of intimidation. When an innocent can randomly be picked up in the street and keeps quiet for fear of physical violence; when a child can be arrested for stealing some tea and end up dead; when an internationally recognized and admired scholar like Saad Eddin Ibrahim is jailed and later fears to return—society is cowed, from top to bottom. And that is just those who do not benefit from the regime. Those who do benefit live in another type of fear: losing favor from the regime and no longer having access to the connections and resources that bring such incredible financial and other benefits. Fear of losing control keeps the core elements of the regime from allowing internal debates between reformers and hardliners from going too far, either in the form of reformers turning to other segments of the political and economic elite for support—not that they exist in any great strength, having been repressed by the regime—or pushing for greater openness politically or economically and a genuine crackdown on the scourge of corruption that goes beyond the occasional show trial. Debate is allowed, and promises can be made, as long as they are not implemented. Differences must not be allowed to become divisions. And the military and security services are ever ready to quash those who actually believe the promises and become indignant when they are not implemented. Ever in the background, the drummed-up fear of the Muslim Brotherhood can be heard.

The ability of the Egyptians to suffer impresses and depresses, but whether they will be willing to continue suffering is far from decided. The forces of globalization have many effects, from the Western tourists shuttled from hotel to museum to monument, to the African migrants for whom even Cairo is an improvement, to the international capital investing in Egypt. The last has some beneficial effects but also the potential of deteriorating life chances for those without the education or the skills—and more crucially in most cases the *wasta,* or "connections"—needed to compete.

The unsettled state of Egyptian society bodes ill. Anger centered on the secret police network, the endemic torture and corruption, and elements of the Westernized elite robbing the country under the guise of liberating its economy and opening it up to foreign investors—all this reminds one, more than anything else, of Iran during the last days of the shah. And like Iran under the shah, and unlike either the Soviet Union or China, Egypt's dynamics are not only internal. That is, the United States plays a significant role in the policies of the Egyptian government.

To be sure, this is rather distinct from the old colonial days in which the British directly controlled the treasury, regularly interfered in government decisions, controlled the Suez Canal and its company, and maintained a significant military presence. Those days of direct colonial control are gone. But in the push and pull toward and away from increased political and economic openness, Washington's voice is heard and listened to, both by the government and by the people. This is hardly surprising, given the considerable amount of money Washington sends Cairo's way. That part of the bargain is more or less sacrosanct, and even while the peace is at best cold, Egypt remains a central element in pursuing Washington's key policy of maintaining stability in the region. But this does not mean that there are not tensions in the relationship, nor that the regime will seek to make Washington happy at the potential risk of undermining itself—and it is hard to believe policy makers in the United States feel otherwise.

One watches, then, the occasional tiffs and spats with something of a gimlet eye: If not exactly pantomime theater, it is almost certainly less than appears at first sight. Thus the regime's limited openness when the Bush administration was on a democracy kick while at the same time talking of developing a nuclear program, which was at first glance useful for internal consumption as indicating independence from the United States but meaningless in reality. Thus the quelling of liberal and secular dissent when Washington's attention was elsewhere. And however unlikely, should the Americans push too hard for democracy and liberalization on the economy, which is to say, push for accountability and transparency in addition to crude privatization, the Mubarak regime can play the fear card yet again: Openness risks the Muslim Brotherhood taking over, they say, pointing to Hamas in the Palestinian territories, Hezbollah in Lebanon, and, of course, the nightmare that theocratic Iran has turned into. The last for a long time seemed to be the biggest trump card of them all, before a new National Intelligence Estimate published in November 2007 found that Iran had abandoned its goal of attaining nuclear weapons back in 2003 and thus allayed fears that war between the United States and Iran was looming on the horizon. Washington nevertheless continues to embrace its allies in the form of "moderate" Sunni Arab regimes like Egypt to drum up support for containing Iran, and to keep in check popular resentment at U.S.-imposed sanctions against that country.

Egyptians historically take a deep interest in regional politics. But closer to home they are more concerned these days with how their country's wealth is being siphoned off in front of their eyes by homegrown fat cats and foreign investors alike, all under what some call the wonders of globalization with all its infamous trickle-down effects in some far-distant future (though note how the fat cats themselves always seem to prefer gratification of the instant kind) and what others damn, in the Canadian journalist Naomi Klein's fashionable phrase, as "shock doctrine." Whatever side one takes on that question, the 1952 revolution seems to be on everyone's mind in Egypt: on that of the regime as it tries to distance itself from the legacy of Nasser while simultaneously milking it for legitimacy and on that of the opposition as it argues that the ideals of the revolution were long since betrayed and that Egypt has effectively come full circle.

Nowhere was this dichotomy more apparent than when the government announced the sale of Banque du Caire, a national institution, to foreigners, causing fury across the political spectrum. Gouda Abdel-Khalek, a professor of economics at Cairo University and member of the leftist Tagammu Party, said he believed the timing of the announcement of the sale coincided deliberately with the fifty-fifth anniversary of the revolution. "In 1952," Abdel-Khalek told a conference organized under the banner "No to Selling Egypt" held at the Press Syndicate in the week after the announcement, "the July Revolution espoused six principles, which included ending the occupation of Egypt and the control of foreign capital. In July 2007, we are being told that these were hollow words, that capital has no borders and the public interest actually lies in selling the bank." By selling so many of Egypt's assets to foreigners, he warned, the government may even be jeopardizing national security. "Even in the most liberal of modern economies, the U.S., a line is drawn," he told the audience, according to *Al-Ahram Weekly;* and he went on to remind them of the way in which U.S. politicians blocked plans by the Dubai-based Ports World company to acquire the operation of six American ports a year earlier because they considered the move a national threat. The sale of the bank added to long-held fears that privatization more generally is heralding the return of colonialism. "Selling this bank will bring back the era of foreign capitulations," independent MP Mustafa Bakri told a meeting of parliament's banking committee. Newspapers were filled with condemnations by employee unions and stories of panicked depositors rushing to withdraw funds from the bank's branches. All this anxiety came in the wake of unprecedented mass demonstrations in six Egyptian governorates that were suffering severe water shortages, which highlighted the dismaying reality that thousands of Egyptians die every year because of a lack of access to clean water—even as massive investment was being made in state-of-the-art sewage and water systems for the new tourist villages and other luxury compounds on the outskirts of cities catering to tourists and the Egyptian superrich. Though the days of direct colonial rule may be gone, the regime's subservience to Washington is a bitter reminder of the past. With Gamal's imminent ascension to the throne, an analogy between the last days of the Farouk monarchy and those of the current regime becomes even more haunting.

In the midst of all this, pushing for yet more privatization at the behest of international monetary organizations risks even more widespread labor unrest and the potential that in the absence of alternative opposition groups the workers could fall, willy-nilly, into the hands of the Muslim Brotherhood. The Brotherhood, of course, was at the forefront of the campaign against the bank sale—"This isn't privatization, it's theft," was how their spokesman laconically described the sell-off—and have long made cleansing Egypt of foreign influence and exploitation a central plank of their political platform. Should such an alliance form, either massive repression or the fall of the regime are the only options. Neither scenario is far-fetched. This dynamic in Egypt, too, appears eerily similar to that in

Iran, another country bedeviled by foreign interference and manipulation for centuries, as the revolution there slowly got under way in the 1970s. For it is important to recall that it was not foreordained that the radical Islamists led by Khomeini would take power in Iran. They were simply one of many groups opposing the shah, and arguably not even the leading or most popular one. Before the revolution, the opposition to the shah's rule was diverse, made up of students, secularists, feminists, Marxists, Islamists, and anti-imperialists. Moreover, the revolution began with wildcat, uncoordinated, and inchoate strikes that built upon each other, were joined by groups with better organization and clearer political goals, and met with a waffling government that neither wanted to give up power nor was capable of quashing the opposition with the full force of the violence at its command. Washington fiddled while Tehran burned, a mess of its own making, and its just punishment, some would even say, for so shamelessly propping up a corrupt leader so hated by his people. Islamists triumphed in the months after the revolution in 1979 because they proved themselves to be the most disciplined and ruthless force. The shah ended up in exile, coincidentally in Egypt; and it was Al-Sadat's praise of the corrupt shah that was one factor that led the Islamists to assassinate him. What goes around certainly comes around in the Middle East, with depressing familiarity. But has Washington, one nevertheless feels compelled to ask, learned any of the lessons?

Most dangerous for the Egyptian regime, the strikes are increasingly setting the agenda, and some workers—it is not yet clear how many—have begun, as an analysis written for the Middle East Report Online in May 2007 points out, "to connect their thin wallets with broader political and economic circumstances: the entrenchment of autocracy; widespread government incompetence and corruption, the regime's subservience to the US and its own inability to offer, or even express an interest in offering, meaningful support for the Palestinian people or meaningful opposition to the war in Iraq; high unemployment and the growing gap between rich and poor." Many Egyptians have begun to speak openly about the need for real change. Public-sector workers are well positioned to play a crucial role if they can organize themselves on a national basis, and the number of strikers does not have to grow more than tenfold for them to reach the kind of figures that have defined popular uprisings of the past. After all, Iran's was the most popular revolution in history, but barely 2 percent of the entire population actually took part in it; the second most popular revolution in history took place in Russia in 1917, when a mere 1.5 percent of the population actively participated.

Nor should either the Egyptian regime or Washington take comfort in what is generally referred to, either dismissively or wishfully, as the apathetic psyche of the Egyptian people. The Orientalist version of Egyptian history has it that Egyptians have been tamed by their experience of being ruled by a pharaoh, and thus conditioned not to question the form and nature of the state, to accept instead that the pharaoh is beyond reproach. People therefore survive by ignoring the alien state, defining their lives according to the alluvial rhythms of the Nile. It would be easy to draw parallels with the present, not least one that equates Mubarak with the pharaoh; he is, after all, the third-longest-ruling Egyptian leader in the past four thousand years. But such an analysis hardly does justice to the vibrant and complex nation-state that is Egypt in the twenty-first century. For a start, the annual flooding of the Nile is a thing of the past, thanks to the High Dam. And the evidence of the past hundred years shows the Egyptians to be far from docile and unconcerned with who rules them or how: a popular revolution against the British (1919), a mass uprising in which half of

Cairo burned (January 1952) followed by the coup d'état (July 1952) itself, and massive food riots that forced Al-Sadat into a humiliating climb down in plans to cut government food subsidies (1977)—not to mention a steady stream of assassinations, mass demonstrations, and terrorist attacks. Such a history hardly speaks, then, of apathy; but still more worrying for the regime, and still more inspiring for those who aim to bring about its demise, is the fact that the gap between both 1919 and 1952, and 1952 and 1977, was about three decades: precisely the period between 1977 and the present. Egypt, this reading of history would suggest, may indeed be ripe for one of its periodic popular uprisings.

Has Washington even considered any of this? The evidence mostly suggests that the answer is no. The Americans therefore find themselves in a number of binds. The overarching one is the desire both for stability and for economic and political reform. In the long term these might be consistent, even mutually reinforcing. But American politicians and policy makers rarely plan for the long term; to be fair, though, that is hardly unique to Americans. In the short term, the desires are not only inconsistent but quite likely work against each other in the Egyptian environment. Maintaining stability means continuing to support Mubarak and his cronies while looking away from the real forces dominating Egyptian politics, the military and the security services. These groups have very little incentive to reform, as they benefit from the status quo, including American aid. The NDP itself also recognizes that reform means giving up some power—as Badrawi pointed out—and not unreasonably they fear that loss of power means diminished control. These are the first, middle, and last pillars of stability, able in the end to stifle change and use force to try and prevent popular unrest from getting out of control. No one doubts their ability to crush dissent, or even a popular uprising; but doing so would hardly get the regime off the hook, because the linchpins of its own reform strategy, privatization and foreign investment, rely for their success, even on their own selfish terms, on internal stability as well.

An American push for genuine economic and political reform, on the other hand, offers at least the potential advantages of economic growth that benefits not only the parasitic elite but also the mass of Egyptians, who currently are protected in their jobs (those who have one) by subsidies that drain the government budget. Were the Egyptian economy stronger, the touts that dominate the tourist areas and the male prostitutes of Luxor would not be as aggressive or both exploitive and exploited. Political reform, meaning increased democracy and transparency, gives potential for the various voices of the pluralistic society of Egypt to participate and push their interests. This would be a radical change from the status quo, wherein the government claims that unity is the paramount value, which is why it gets angry when anyone points out that minorities exist, and why it claims to represent the best interests of the Egyptian people—all the while refusing to put that claim to the test of free and open elections.

These conflicting goals were captured in the rather bizarre experience of one Hisham Kassem, an Egyptian human rights activist who, in October 2007, was one of four international activists given the prestigious Democracy Award of the National Endowment for Democracy. Kassem found the experience woefully depressing. "To see the president of the United States in person and his more or less lack of interest in what is happening politically in Egypt left me without any doubt that this whole [democracy] program was over," he told Reuters after collecting his award. Kassem said that although the president asked about reformers in the ruling NDP (to which he replied: "Sorry, there are no reformers at the NDP"), Bush was mainly interested in the position of Islamists in Egypt. Kassem made clear that the government had made it impossible for secular political movements to operate, leaving the field open to the Islamists: "There is no alternative now for the people, given that Islamists operate out of mosques while secular political parties are not allowed to operate at all." With the difficult economic situation, he added, "I am worried that Egypt will become a theocracy by 2010." Apparently that comment finally got Bush's full attention, and he seemed rather perplexed that American policy was not working, noting: "We give your country $2 billion a year in order to keep it stable and prevent it from turning into a theocracy." He looked, Kassem said, quite dismayed.

Some would argue that Kassem did himself no favors in meeting with Bush and his top advisors. For the unfortunate reality is that the American push for democracy is now perceived as having been insincere at best, hypocritical at worst. Which is hardly surprising, when for the president the purpose of the payoff to Mubarak's regime is stability rather than reform. One effect of the inconsistency in American policy is that any attempt to help democratically inclined individuals and movements in Egypt has the undesired effect of diminishing their support in their own constituencies. That is, they are considered guilty by association. Kassem may have been more likely to win support in Egypt itself for his cause had he refused to meet Bush in the first place. For many of the secular reformists are hardly enamored of Americans, which was clear to me when, at the height of the Cairo Spring in early 2004, I met with a number of them, including Ahmed Said Al-Islam, the head of an Egyptian human rights group called the Hisham Mubarak Law Center. He should have been feeling empowered by the pressure from the United States to bring about what Islam has been trying to highlight for a decade: the need for greater democracy, freedom, and accountability. Instead, Islam told me that he and other reformers remained deeply skeptical of, if not openly hostile to, America's role in the region. "The war on terror is undermining democracy advocates and strengthening Arab dictatorships," he said in his home, a stone's throw from Cairo University. "The latter are using it to put off reforms and arguing that being pro-reform means siding with the enemies of the state." There was plenty of proof to back up Islam's argument. The week I met him *Al-Osbou* newspaper, which is close to Mubarak's ruling party, ran an article titled "Washington's Plan for Egypt," which claimed that America's aim was to appoint a Coptic Christian as vice president and cancel Article Two of the Constitution (which states that Islamic sharia law is the bedrock of the legal system). Meanwhile, the pro-government *Rose Al-Youssef* weekly was accusing Saad Eddin Ibrahim of "collaborating with the U.S. and Israel to defame Egypt's image." The broader anti-U.S. climate was facilitating the orchestrated backlash. "The war on Iraq has put the reform agenda back in several ways, and triggered a sort of vendetta against the United States. That is spilling over into a vendetta against the West as a whole," Hani Shakrallah, then managing editor of *Al-Ahram Weekly,* told me at the time. "With the Patriot Act, Guantánamo Bay, Abu Ghraib, and [the destruction of] Fallujah, no one in the Arab world can now listen to Americans advocating democracy with a straight face." The further paradox is that even where there is renewed movement for reform, it is almost all in a direction that challenges U.S. interests: Promoting democracy across the Arab world, even in a sound-bite fashion, was always going to mean Arabs would be likely to express stronger criticism of Israel and America's related Middle East policies.

The United Nations Development Program lent its name to the 2003 Arab Human Development Report on governance in the Arab world despite U.S. objections to parts of the text. Its principal author, the Egyptian intellectual Nader Fergany, told me in his Cairo office that the study had infuriated Arab regimes and the United States in equal measure. "One reason is that it has rather strong criticism of the American occupation of Iraq," he said. "And it argues that the way the so-called war on terror has been waged has definitely resulted in further restrictions of freedom in Arab countries." This report had to approach the "bull's-eye," he added. "It was natural that it would not be received warmly by bad governance regimes—including the United States, which is a very clear case of a bad governance regime that is not very supportive of freedom." It now seems almost surreal that the Bush administration used the 2002 Arab Human Development Report as the basis for its first detailed proposals on reform in the Arab world. The United States is, it is clear, caught between not only the Islamist opposition and the regime, but also the secular opposition (or what remains of it) and the regime.

One is tempted, in however humble a capacity, to offer Washington advice in this context, not least because in January 2009 the present American president will leave office, part of a democratic process that the American people may decide is to be a mass routing of what remains of the neoconservative advisors who surrounded Bush. However, there is nothing at this stage to suggest that the person who replaces Bush, whether Democrat or Republican, will have anything new or original to contribute to American foreign policy in the region, or will be willing to listen to different voices. At the same time, it should now be crystal clear to all of the candidates that crude military interventionism, be it preemptive or otherwise, is a recipe only for disaster in the region, the blowback unacceptable not just in terms of local civilian deaths and injuries (in addition to the deaths and injuries of U.S. troops) but in terms, too, of the resentment such wars create among the Arab masses, and the concomitant opportunities they offer for mainstream Islamist groupings like the Muslim Brotherhood to shore up their support.

A different approach to Egypt would take heart from the fact that the Muslim Brotherhood has made only limited inroads into the mainstream since the 1920s; that Islam as practiced by most Egyptians is essentially Sufi in nature and by default therefore intolerant of extremist Sunni doctrine (let alone Al-Qaeda-inspired violence); that Muslims and Christians in Egypt are overwhelmingly proud of their shared history and for the most part continue to live as one and participate in each other's festivals and religious holidays; that, notwithstanding the anti-Israeli propaganda orchestrated by the regime, Egyptians are quite happy to work with Israelis so long as the terms are just and fair (as evidenced in the Israeli "qualifying industrial zones" established in Egypt) and the plight of their fellow Arabs in Palestinine is given more than just token acknowledgment; and that there remains such admiration for American and European freedom, if not politics, that year in and year out many Egyptians are willing to risk their liberty or even their lives for the briefest of opportunities to taste it for themselves.

The key, of course, is the $2 billion the United States gives Egypt annually in aid, which should unequivocally be tied to progress on reform and with a clear threat that the money will be diverted to grassroots projects in Egypt that promote democracy if reform is not only said to be happening but seen to be happening as well. Washington should get something for its money; and what does Washington really have to lose by following such a course? The Mubarak regime is hardly likely to hand over power to the Muslim Brotherhood when its bluff is called, or stoke up popular anger to the extent that it might get out of control. Who among the Egyptians anyway would not be happy that the regime is getting a metaphorical slap in the face, bearing in mind the very physical slaps and worse so many of them have to suffer at the hands of the regime's thugs every day? Israel, meanwhile, is so superior militarily to Egypt that an attack by the latter on the former would be nothing short of suicide. Regionally, Egypt's influence is

also greatly diminished. From Palestine to Iraq, Lebanon to Syria, and crucially Iran, it is Saudi Arabia that is now calling the shots, and there is no
more reliable Washington ally in the Arab world than the House of Saud—
an ally, moreover, pretty much immune to pressure from Washington when
the price of oil is hovering at all-time highs. Under such pressure, the
Egyptian regime would have no choice but to introduce meaningful reforms, however slowly. Inching forward is preferable to no movement at all.

For two hundred years, Egypt has steered a course between the two
poles of the East and the West. Ordinary Egyptians are Washington's natural allies, if they can see real benefit to themselves in the alliance. For Washington to abandon the Egyptian people by letting things fester, with all the
risk that entails of bringing the Muslim Brotherhood to power, as though
the Egyptian people deserve nothing better and want nothing more, as
many Washington-based policy analysts seem increasingly to advocate,
would be more than just a betrayal of what has historically been the Arab
world's most vibrant and diverse culture: It would also sound the death
knell for democracy and pluralism throughout the region. In short, Washington must think long-term, slowly reassessing its support for Egypt's dictator while doing its utmost to resolve the Palestinian issue, which he
exploits to deflect attention from his own considerable shortcomings. The
United States must urge economic reforms that address the very valid concerns of the Egyptian masses.

The United States has a long history of involvement in the Middle
East, and rarely have policies gone the way Washington intended—even if
we assume the best of intentions. One of the dominant buildings in the
Cairo skyline is the Cairo Tower. It is just one of the legacies of the American effort to get Nasser on their side. One story goes that it was built with
money given, effectively as a bribe, by Kermit (Kim) Roosevelt, the legendary CIA operative (who played, incidentally, a central role in the

restoration of the shah in 1953). The building is known as Nasser's Prick, for Nasser took the money and went on his merry way, pursuing his own policies. In a sense, the current government is likewise giving the Americans the finger, and the basic bargain was neatly summarized by Bush in his meeting with Kassem in Washington. With American prestige in the region so low, given the atrocious failure in Iraq and the lack of progress in Palestinian-Israeli peace negotiations, Mubarak feels that the Americans in the short term have few options, and little desire to press too far. The result is that the regime believes there is every reason to think the status quo will continue.

⌣

In the fall of 2007, the NDP held elections for its top leadership, and during the run-up the consensus was that Mubarak would win handily; in a prediction with greater foresight than the famous "Dewey Beats Truman," the state-owned *Al-Gomhouriya* newspaper headlined an article "Mubarak Will Be Elected Unanimously." He was, of course; and Gamal was moved up in the party's hierarchy, making him, according to the Byzantine official regulations, finally eligible to stand for the presidency in his own right. Authoritarian regimes may be dull, but at least they are predictable. And that, sadly, appears to be what Washington wants. The problem, however, is politics is rarely predictable, least of all in the Middle East. While one should never underestimate the ability of the Mubarak regime to muddle along, the underlying ferment among workers and others is hardly a reason for optimism. Nor is the regime laying the groundwork for increasing openness by, for example, pursuing policies that are likely to increase the people's support, even if not unanimous. Bereft of ideas or ideology or symbols that resonate with the people, the regime leaves problems unsolved and festering.

And who is there to pick up the pieces? The Muslim Brotherhood. I am not saying that the Muslim Brotherhood is particularly popular, let alone that it has sensible (or viable) solutions. Rather, as the only organized opposition, it is if only by default the strongest one. The founder of the Muslim Brotherhood, Hassan Al-Banna, outlined a strategy of patience that had three stages for taking power: the propaganda stage (preparation), the organization stage (aimed at educating the people), and finally, the action stage (where power is seized). General and vague as that scheme might be, and indeed as most analyses of the Muslim Brotherhood tend to be, it does imply practical measures, and it can rather fairly be said that the Muslim Brotherhood is in effect at the second stage—evidenced by their focus on education and culture, or more precisely the eradication of all forms of such that do not comply with its Islamist dogma.

What is equally apparent is that the Muslim Brotherhood learns from the experiences of others. In the fall of 2007, their official Web page made positive reference to a BBC article that laid out the conditions most likely to lead to popular unrest and overthrow of a government, using as an example the unfortunate experience of Myanmar (Burma) under the military regime. Among the key factors identified as likely to lead to regime change: widespread public protests, bringing in many different social and economic groups; an opposition leadership with clear ideas around which people can rally; the ability to use the media in some form to get a message across; a mechanism for undermining the existing regime, whether by internal coup in the case of a military junta, the emergence of reformers, or the simple exhaustion of an existing government leading to its collapse. The excited Muslim Brotherhood activist who brought attention to the article asked his fellow Islamists on their Web site: "In Egypt, can it be implemented?" The question was posited, one got the impression, more than just rhetorically.

A NOTE ON SOURCES

This book is primarily aimed at the general reader. I have therefore not included footnotes or other academic clutter, instead working references into the text. However, I would like to acknowledge here some secondary sources that were particularly useful. In sketching the history of modern Egypt between Napoleon's invasion in 1798 and the 1952 coup led by the Free Officers, I relied mainly on *Egypt's Belle Époque* (1989) by Trevor Mostyn, *Modern Egypt: The Formation of a Nation-State* (2004) by Arthur Goldschmidt Jr., and *Egypt: A Short History* (2000) by James Jankowski. The quotation by Awad Al-Mor in chapter 1 is taken from Maye Kassem's *Egyptian Politics: The Dynamics of Authoritarian Rule* (2004). In chapter 4 for some background material I have drawn on "Settling for More or Less?" by Cache Seel, *Egypt Today*, June 2006. I have found Barry Rubin's *Islamic Fundamentalism in Egyptian Politics* (updated, 2002) the most useful guide to the history and development of Islamist groups in Egypt.

INDEX

the pyramids and, 149
of religion, 77, 79
of tourism, 149–50, 200
Western culture and, 49, 50
cotton exports, 25, 87
coup of 1952, 2, 131, 169, 211, 217,
 221, 231
 cultural reassessment of, 10
 failure of, 20–21
 fiftieth anniversary of, 11, 16
 imitations inspired by, 12
 legacy of, 10–17
 U.S. knowledge of, 12
culture, control of, 61–63

Dahab, terrorist attacks in, 102, 103
Al-Deen, Abdul-Halim Nour, 152
democracy:
 Egypt ruled by parliamentary, 20,
 26, 48
 judgment of, 19
 Islam and, 18
 Islamism and, 64–65
 Nasser's declarations of, 12, 19
 "spreading," 68–69, 223–24
demographics, Egyptian, 37–38, 40, 83,
 85, 109–10, 140
Diab, Salah, 162
diversity, Egyptian, 81–84, 222, 227
Doing Business 2008, 164, 167
Durrell, Lawrence, 38–39

Economist (magazine), 11
Education for Employment
 Foundation, 209
education system:

for Bedouins, 109–10
failure of, 2, 8, 20, 32–33, 208–209
 under Mohammed Ali, 25
 under Mubarak, 32
 under Nasser, 10, 29, 208
 tutors and, 44
Egypt Today (magazine), 6, 8, 98, 99,
 231
Egyptian Museum, 148, 150–52
Egyptian Organization for Human
 Rights (EOHR), 127, 140
Eissa, Ibrahim, 140
El-Gamal, Rania, 144–45
elections, political, 41, 58, 203, 210
 of 2000, 49
 of 2005, 35, 49, 56–57, 65–68, 162
 of 2007, 228
 Bedouin vote in, 111
 corruption and, 21, 82
 free and open, 210, 222
 Islamism and, 65–67, 77, 98
Elembaby, Saad, 190
emergency law/rule, 15, 56, 59, 131,
 135, 140
Emigrant, The (film), 170
emigration, 84, 170–72
extraordinary rendition, 130, 132,
 134

Farouk, King, 14, 18, 23, 31, 36, 54, 169,
 211, 218
Fatimid dynasty, 88
Fawakhriya (Bedouin tribe), 101
Fayad, Susan, 143
female genital mutilation, 37
Fergany, Nader, 224